Information Literacy and Libraries in the Age of Fake News

Information Literacy and Libraries in the Age of Fake News

Denise E. Agosto, Editor

LIBRARIES UNLIMITED™
An Imprint of ABC-CLIO, LLC
Santa Barbara, California • Denver, Colorado

Library of Congress Cataloging-in-Publication Data

Names: Agosto, Denise E., editor.
Title: Information literacy and libraries in the age of fake news / Denise E.
  Agosto, editor.
Description: Santa Barbara : Libraries Unlimited, [2018] | Includes
  bibliographical references and index.
Identifiers: LCCN 2018028659 (print) | LCCN 2018042542 (ebook) | ISBN
  9781440864193 (ebook) | ISBN 9781440864186 (paperback : acid-free paper)
Subjects: LCSH: Information literacy. | Information literacy—Study and
  teaching—United States. | Media literacy. | Media literacy—Study and
  teaching—United States. | Libraries and education—United States. |
  Fake news—United States.
Classification: LCC ZA3075 (ebook) | LCC ZA3075 .I53275 2018 (print) |
  DDC 028.7—dc23
LC record available at https://lccn.loc.gov/2018028659

ISBN: 978-1-4408-6418-6 (paperback)
        978-1-4408-6419-3 (ebook)

22 21 20 19 18   1 2 3 4 5

This book is also available as an eBook.

Libraries Unlimited
An Imprint of ABC-CLIO, LLC

ABC-CLIO, LLC
130 Cremona Drive, P.O. Box 1911
Santa Barbara, California 93116-1911
www.abc-clio.com

This book is printed on acid-free paper ∞

Manufactured in the United States of America

This book is dedicated to David and Rachel.
And to a kinder, more thoughtful, better-informed
future for our world.

Contents

Foreword

While a "single event" is often identified as an event that "changed the world" or "changed the course of history," one can't help but think that the identification of that event as "world-" or "life-changing" must be hyperbole. How can events, actions, activities, and speeches have such an impact that our world shifts or our work changes or the nature of what we believe is altered? It *is* so, however, and this past year—with the advent of "fake news," our profession was forced—no matter what we believe individually—not only to begin to review and revise our core practices but also to address our definitions, our processes, our products and tools, or, more simply put, our entire information literacy curriculum.

Just some evidence of the profession stepping in can be found in our Web guides. In the spring of 2017, hundreds of fake news pathfinders had appeared with steady, significant monthly increases in online content designed to address the continuing issues. Almost a year later, over 7,000 specific fake news pages exist. In addition, general "critical thinking" content has grown, with over 15,000 pages for both general and discipline-specific content now available online for teaching and learning.

Obviously, however, online content is not enough. Now and going forward, we have many difficult issues to deal with for teaching people how to identify, evaluate, and apply—including dealing with attempts to rewrite history, to interpret reality, to ignore diversity, equity and inclusion, and to shatter our standards and applications for authority and credibility. Specifically:

- What and who defines authority or credibility? Education? Experience? A title? Holding an office (elected or appointed?) Is the source identified—the actual source?

- How does and how should currency play a role in our choices and decision making? Is the latest or last information the best in all disciplines or situations?
- What *is* the underlying evidence for an issue? What makes evidence, evidence?
- What purpose is served by content? Why was it created?

Are we in the worst situation in U.S. history for learning how to make our own choices and informed decisions? There is much debate on that question, and while I don't have the answer, I do know that all of us must take the lead in the debate not only on teaching others how to listen, evaluate, and choose but also on the importance of critically questioning ideas, proposals, stories, and the news.

Although it was and is exciting to be at the center (and often the forefront) of change, when—literally—our reality is called into question, it is of critical importance that we take great care so that all of our communities understand that—no matter the social or political leanings—*all* people benefit from the truth.

Julie B. Todaro, DLS
2016–2017 President of the American Library Association

ONE

An Introduction to Information Literacy and Libraries in the Age of Fake News

Denise E. Agosto

> When it comes to libraries and issues of information accuracy and authenticity, it's all about education. Libraries of all types—public, corporate, academic, special, government, and school—are fundamentally educational organizations. We teach our community members about information. That is our special contribution to bettering society.

In many ways, the 2016 U.S. presidential election was a watershed event. It marked the first time a woman had served as a presidential candidate on a major party ticket. It brought to light the potentially misleading nature of large-scale polling data. And it put the term "fake news" into the daily lexicon, not just in the United States but around the world.

The rise of fake news stories—false or misleading stories that are "masterfully manipulated to look like credible journalistic reports [and that] are easily spread online to large audiences willing to believe the fictions and spread the word" (Holan 2016)—are correlated with a rise in widespread public reliance on online sources for news. In fact, the Pulitzer Prize–winning Web site Politifact named fake news its 2016 "lie of the year":

Fake news: Hillary Clinton is running a child sex ring out of a pizza shop.

Fake news: Democrats want to impose Islamic law in Florida.

Fake news: Thousands of people at a Donald Trump rally in Manhattan chanted, 'We hate Muslims, we hate blacks, we want our great country back.'

None of those stories—and there are so many more like them—is remotely true. (Holan 2016)

The fake news discourse was and is especially relevant to libraries. Librarians have long been in the business of teaching users how to think critically and how to evaluate information. Although school and academic librarians have been the most visible promoters of critical thinking and information evaluation as fundamental to their services, both concepts are core aspects of public, special, and government library services as well. This book revolves around the idea that librarians have both the opportunity and the responsibility to teach their communities how to determine whether the information they encounter online is accurate, reliable, and worthy of being shared.

SOME BACKGROUND: NEWS AND OTHER INFORMATION IN TODAY'S COMPLEX INFORMATION ENVIRONMENT

In the wake of the online information explosion, information is produced in many ways that go beyond the traditional writer-editor-publication process that used to underlie the dissemination of most news. Much of the information on the Web today is user-produced, as opposed to being written by professional writers, researchers, news reporters, and academics. Although print newspapers used to be a main source of daily information for most U.S. adults, today only about 20 percent of U.S. adults "often" get news from a print newspaper (Mitchell, Gottfried, Barthel, and Shearer 2016).

Instead, most people now get news and other daily information from an ever widening array of online information sources. Nearly twice as many U.S. adults get their news from online sources as print newspapers, and more than three-quarters of U.S. adults use Web sites, apps, or social media as sources of news or other information (Mitchell et al. 2016).

For many people, social media in particular is playing a large and growing role in their monitoring of what's going on in their communities at the local, national, and global levels. An estimated 14 percent of U.S. adults relied on social media as their *most important* source of news about the 2016 U.S. presidential election (Allcott and Gentzkow 2017). This means that the types of news their friends chose to share online likely shaped their opinions of the election and possibly influenced their voting choices. Fourteen percent of U.S. adults may not seem that significant, but it translates into more than 30 million potential voters in an election in which about 137 million votes in total were cast (United States Election Project 2016).

Reliable information can be transmitted in any format, from print newspapers to mobile news apps to everyday people's social media posts. So why does it matter what format people use to get news? The answer lies in the ways that information is created, vetted (or not), and distributed. Although in the primarily paper-based information world of decades past, most widely available information was vetted by professional editors or other experts, much of the information available online today is not. The result is a groundswell of unverified and unverifiable information being passed around online, not just intentionally created fake news but unintentionally false or misleading information as well.

Unfortunately, many users have trouble understanding where the information they find online comes from and knowing which information to trust and not to trust. A large-scale Stanford University study found widespread confusion among middle school, high school, and college students when it came to assessing online information. It concluded, "Overall, young people's ability to reason about the information on the Internet can be summed up in one word: bleak" (Wineburg, McGrew, Breakstone, and Ortega 2016). The Stanford study further concluded, "When it comes to evaluating information that flows through social media channels, [students] are easily duped" (Wineburg et al. 2016). Students in the study had difficulty differentiating between news content and advertising content, and most lacked an understanding of how biased perspectives affect news and other information messages. Many adults have similar difficulty assessing information that they encounter online.

A BIT MORE BACKGROUND: HOW WE SPEND OUR TIME ONLINE

As of early 2018, nearly 90 percent of U.S. citizens regularly go online. Over three-quarters (77%) own a smartphone, and almost three-quarters (73%) have broadband service at home. Among all U.S. adults, online users or not, 69 percent use some type of social media, with 86 percent of U.S. adults ages 18–29 using social media (Pew Research Center 2018a).

Facebook is still by far the most popular social network in the United States, with 68 percent of U.S. adults using it in 2018. The next most popular are Instagram (35%), Pinterest (29%), Snapchat (27%), and LinkedIn (25%) (Pew Research Center 2018b).

Thinking about all screen media (computers, cell phones, TV, tablets, etc.) together, the average U.S. adult spends over 10 hours a day looking at screens (Howard 2016). There's no way around it: That's a lot of time spent online. It means that time spent reading paper books, reading paper newspapers, and engaging in other activities we traditionally associate with libraries has been reduced for many people in order to leave so much time to be spent online.

Still, book reading is far from dead. About three-quarters (74%) of U.S. adults read at least one book in whole or in part in print, e-book, or audio book form during 2015 (Perrin 2018). And although e-book use is down over the past couple of years, paper book purchases are on the rise (Kottasová 2017).

Just as people are still reading books, for the most part most people's core life activities haven't changed all that much despite the large amounts of time they spend online. Most people still spend the bulk of their time working, sleeping, eating, shopping, spending time with family and friends, engaging in leisure pursuits, and so on—but much of this activity has moved online, especially communication activities. Many people are communicating with more people more frequently than they did in past decades, and much of this activity is taking place in social media, where real news headlines, fake news headlines, and a barrage of other information bombards them every day.

How does spending all this time online affect how people look for information? A common finding across the information research from the 20th century was that people tended to turn to other people first as sources of information for both work and personal information needs, turning much less frequently to nonhuman information sources (books, magazines, etc.). This is still largely true, but for small information needs—such as looking up quick facts—often the first choice today is to consult the Internet/Web through a quick search on a cell phone or other device.

For larger needs—such as advice for a work issue or information to help solve a personal problem—often other people are still users' first choices for information. However, now users often connect to these other people via networked means, such as posting a question to social media or texting a friend for advice. For example, research by Forte, Dickard, Magee, and Agosto (2014) showed that high school students frequently turned to social media to ask their peers questions related to school, such as scheduling and homework questions. Typically within minutes they would receive answers to their questions, as large numbers of their classmates were also online in the same environments. The ability to more readily access others via social media is a huge benefit of these social media, but the flotsam and jetsam of fake information floating around in the media can also negatively impact people's lives.

THE EFFECTS OF FAKE NEWS

Fake news and other false or misleading information online can have a very real influence on society. For example, conspiracy theorist Alex Jones formally apologized for creating a video to promote the Hillary Clinton child sex ring in the pizza shop story ("Pizzagate") previously referenced (Farhi 2017), but he apologized only after his video about it had already spread wildly, garnering nearly a half million views. At the same time, there were also almost a million and a half #Pizzagate tweets on Twitter (Robb 2017), not to mention the hundreds of thousands or possibly even millions of other mentions and posts across the Internet. No doubt many of those who heard about the story believed it and shared it among their personal networks on social media. For some of these people, the story likely influenced their voting behaviors and their broader political beliefs, and even though the story has been shown to be entirely false, some people are probably still believers.

But why would people continue to believe a fake story? They may simply not have heard that it was retracted, and, more importantly, there are complex reasons why they would have believed the story in the first place. One reason is that, as is typical of fake news, Jones's video was presented in a highly emotionally charged style, whereas the retraction was generally presented as fact and reported with journalistic dispassion. People tend to find emotional content much more compelling than facts or statistics (Sharot 2017). Moreover, confirmation bias—the human tendency to believe information that agrees with or confirms a person's beliefs or biases (Nickerson 1998)—also plays a role in people's acceptance of fake news. In the Pizzagate case, people who already had a negative impression of Hillary Clinton were likely to hear the story, believe it, and have their negative impressions strengthened, especially if they heard the story from a trusted friend or family member.

Of course, it was not just individuals who were sharing election-related information in social media during the run-up to the 2016 U.S. presidential election. Many news outlets, both legitimate and questionable, also chose to share election information on social media, reaching potential voters within their personal social spheres. A significant number of these so-called news outlets were fake news creators who circulated inaccurate news solely to promote their own agendas, or they were contractors who issued erroneous stories as paid work to promote someone else's agenda.

That said, fake news is not a new phenomenon. It did not originate during the 2016 election cycle; rather, false and misleading news can be traced back more than a century to the era of yellow journalism and perhaps much further back. Nonetheless, with the recent surge of people participating in social media, the amount and influence of fake news have burgeoned.

Often the motivation behind fake news is purely profit. If people click on fake news headlines, fake news writers can earn advertising money with each click. Fake news is big business. Individual creators of fake news stories can make thousands of dollars per month from advertising revenue (Ohlheiser 2016). This means that fake newswriters—and even "real" newswriters—are heavily motivated to create the most sensational headlines that they can, and in most cases they can create fake news with impunity—there is no oversight agency to prevent them from doing it.

Although the 2016 election brought a spotlight to the issue, fake news addresses many events and topics beyond elections. Users must understand how to identify its media platforms and topics: "Fake news is not just an election issue; it is an information and media literacy [issue]. . . . Access to the Internet means nothing if someone is unable to discern between fact and conspiracy theory" (Alverez 2016). As such, the influence of fake news is far-reaching, and librarians must make combating its effects a core goal of their work not just during elections but at all times. This means that it's more important than ever for librarians and other information professionals to teach users how to think critically and how to evaluate information—how to know which information to trust and rely on to support the full range of activities in their personal, educational, professional, and social lives.

LIBRARIANS AS INFORMATION EXPERTS AND INFORMATION EDUCATORS

A main theme—perhaps *the* main theme—of this book is that librarians and other information professionals are information experts and information educators. Even librarians who don't think of themselves as technologically inclined have much to teach their communities about the Internet, the Web, and online information. The very nature of library and information science education and of library work means that librarians know much more about how information is created, distributed, and used than most members of the public, and they are perfectly positioned to teach their users what they know and how to apply that knowledge to everyday life contexts.

Most librarians are familiar with the concept of information literacy: "the set of integrated abilities encompassing the reflective discovery of information, the understanding of how information is produced and valued, and the use of information in creating new knowledge and participating ethically in communities of learning" (ACRL 2016). Strong information skills are crucial for effective participation in a democratic society, both for informed voting and for impactful civic engagement. As Atifete Jahjaga, the first female president of Kosovo, said: "Democracy must be built through open societies that share information. When there is information, there is enlightenment. When there is debate, there are solutions. . . . People must have access to information for informed debate" (Jahjaga 2012).

The ACRL *Framework for Information Literacy for Higher Education* (ACRL 2016) was designed with higher education in mind, but it offers a framework for librarians working in all contexts to teach their community members about the complicated nature of information writ large, as well as how to approach information with a critical eye. The *Framework* includes six concepts that are central to information literacy. These include the importance of understanding that:

1. information authority varies as context varies;
2. information is created through many different processes;
3. information in itself has value;
4. research is an inquiry-driven process;
5. scholarship should be thought of in terms of an ongoing conversation and discussion; and
6. the process of searching for information involves strategic exploration (ACRL 2016).

These six concepts can serve as a guide for effective programming and education relating to fake news and information literacy.

In addition to adopting an information literacy approach, librarians can teach their community members to approach information critically. They can teach their users about the many different ways in which information is created and to "view authority with an attitude of informed skepticism and an openness to new perspectives, additional voices, and changes in schools of thought" (PALNI 2017).

THE IMPLICATIONS FOR THE EVOLVING ROLES OF LIBRARIES AND LIBRARIANS

In past decades, arguably the main role of public, academic, special, and school librarians was providing members of their communities with access to information (Spratt and Agosto 2017, p. 17). In today's world, where the majority of people in the United States have daily access to smartphones, laptops, and other networked devices, information access is much less of an issue for most people. The pressing issue has become how to determine the accuracy and authority of online information—what information sources users can and should trust in their daily lives. This means that librarians' role in teaching users about information evaluation and thinking critically about the information they encounter online is more important than ever. When people ask, "Why do we need libraries and librarians now that everything is online?" A good answer is that librarians can play the role of information educators, helping to empower their users, not just to access information but *to understand which information to trust.*

Many libraries are stepping into this role and acknowledging the collective role of librarians in working to create a more educated, more information-savvy population. The U.S. public generally holds their libraries in high regard, placing librarians in positions with strong potential influence in the area of information education: "In a world where faith in American institutions is crumbling, people still trust libraries. And just as they have with every other monumental development in American history—whether technological, cultural, or existential—librarians are already preparing for how to evolve to serve us best" (Fuller 2017).

Libraries of all types can create educational programming to teach users how to evaluate information sources, thereby addressing the need for a more informed, more critical society. Several U.S. public libraries have begun offering programs to teach users about fake news. For example, the Longmont Library (Colorado) created a program entitled The Real Story behind Fake News. It featured a local university professor discussing examples of fake news and teaching program participants how to identify "real" and "fake" news and news sources (Tinsley 2017).

Specific program ideas and guidelines abound for teaching users how to evaluate information accuracy and authenticity. Librarians can select sets of evaluation recommendations that are right for their particular user groups and offer hands-on evaluation sessions in the library. Or they can take their lessons out into their communities and meet users where they live, work, and play.

As previously explained, librarians' roles are increasingly moving toward teaching users how to navigate the world of online information, and critical thinking and information literacy are even more important for success in today's society than in the past. Consequently, much of the focus of library services has moved away from library collections out to the broader world of networked information, and we can expect this shift in focus to continue.

This volume is intended to further this shift in focus. It begins with a set of chapters explaining key concepts in understanding the fake news phenomenon and its impact on society, including the history of fake news going back to its origins in the yellow journalism of the 19th century; critical literacy as a key concept in fighting misinformation and disinformation; connections among poverty, social inequity, and information literacy; and free speech and intellectual freedom in the age of fake news. The second set of chapters focuses on practical approaches that librarians can take to educate their communities about critical approaches to information literacy. These include evaluation techniques; resource development; sample model programs in public, school, and academic libraries; and ideas for developing fake news and critical literacy curricula.

CONCLUDING THOUGHTS: AN EYE TOWARD THE FUTURE

When it comes to libraries and issues of information accuracy and authenticity, it's all about education. Libraries of all types—public, corporate, academic, special, government, and school—are *fundamentally* educational organizations. We teach our community members about information. That is our special contribution to bettering society. Remember: Librarians are information educators, and we can work to make our community members better educated, as well as more thoughtful future information creators, users, and sharers.

REFERENCES

ACRL (Association of College & Research Libraries). *Framework for Information Literacy for Higher Education*, 11 January 2016. http://www.ala.org/acrl/standards/ilframework.

Allcott, Hunt, and Matthew Gentzkow. "Social Media and Fake News in the 2016 Election." *Journal of Economic Perspectives* 31, no. 2 (2017): 211–236. https://web.stanford.edu/~gentzkow/research/fake news.pdf.

Alvarez, Barbara. "Public Libraries in the Age of Fake News." *Public Libraries* 55, no. 6 (2016): 24–27.

Farhi, Paul. "Conspiracy Theorist Alex Jones Apologizes for Role in Fake "Pizzagate" Story." *Washington Post*, 24 March 2017. http://www .chicagotribune.com/news/nationworld/ct-alex-jones-pizzagate -apology-20170324-story.html.

Forte, Andrea, Michael Dickard, Rachel Magee, and Denise E. Agosto. "What Do Teens Ask Their Online Social Networks? Social Search Practices among High School Students." In *Proceedings of the 17th ACM Conference on Computer Supported Cooperative Work & Social Computing*, 28–37. New York: Association for Computing Machinery, 2014.

Fuller, Jaime. "In Trump's America, Activist Librarians Who Won't be Shushed." MTV News, 19 January 2017. www.mtv.com/news/297 3842/in-trumps-america-activist-librarians-who-wont-be-shushed/.

Holan, Angie Drobnic. "2016 Lie of the Year: Fake News." *Politifact*, 13 December 2016. http://www.politifact.com/truth-o-meter/article /2016/dec/13/2016-lie-year-fake-news.

Howard, Jacqueline. "Americans Devote More Than 10 Hours a Day to Screen Time, and Growing." CNN, 29 July 2016. http://www.cnn .com/2016/06/30/health/americans-screen-time-nielsen.

Jahjaga, Atifete. "Kosovar President Atifete Jahjaga: The Four Key Ingre-dients for Peace." *The Hill*, 14 June 2012. http://thehill.com/policy /international/232703-kosovar-president-atifete-jahjaga-the-four -key-ingredients-for-peace.

Kottasová, Ivana. "Real Books Are Back. E-Book Sales Plunge Nearly 20%." CNN, 27 April 2017. http://money.cnn.com/2017/04/27/media /ebooks-sales-real-books/index.html.

Mitchell, Amy, Jeffrey Gottfried, Michael Barthel, and Elisa Shearer. "Path-ways to News." Pew Research Center, 7 July 2016. http://www .journalism.org/2016/07/07/pathways-to-news.

Nickerson, Raymond S. "Confirmation Bias: A Ubiquitous Phenomenon in Many Guises." *Review of General Psychology* 2, no. 2 (1998): 737–759.

Ohlheiser, Abby. "This Is How Facebook's Fake-News Writers Make Money." *Washington Post*, 18 November 2016. https://www.washington post.com/news/the-intersect/wp/2016/11/18/this-is-how-the -internets-fake-news-writers-make-money/?utm_term=.43c3d0 46a1e5.

PALNI. *Framework for Information Literacy for Higher Education*, 6 March 2017. http://libguides.palni.edu/c.php?g=185459&p=1224981.

Perrin, Andrew. "Who Doesn't Read Books in America?" Pew Research Center, 23 March 2018. http://www.pewresearch.org/fact-tank/2018 /03/23/who-doesnt-read-books-in-america/.

Pew Research Center. "Internet/Broadband Factsheet," 5 February 2018a. http://www.pewinternet.org/fact-sheet/internet-broadband.

Pew Research Center. "Social Media Factsheet," 5 February 2018b. http:// www.pewinternet.org/fact-sheet/social-media.

Robb, Amanda. "Anatomy of a Fake News Scandal." *Rolling Stone*, 16 November 2017. https://www.rollingstone.com/politics/news/pizza gate-anatomy-of-a-fake-news-scandal-w511904.

Sharot, Tali. *The Influential Mind: What the Brain Reveals about Our Power to Change Others*. New York: Henry Holt & Company, 2017.

Spratt, Hannah, and Denise E. Agosto. "Fighting Fake News: Because We All Deserve the Truth." *Young Adult Library Services* 15, no. 4 (2017): 17–21.

Tinsley, Erica. "Longmont Library Creates Program to Combat Fake News." *Coloradoan*, 27 January 2017. http://www.coloradoan.com/story /news/local/colorado/2017/01/27/longmont-library-creates-program -combat-fake-news/97171968.

United States Election Project. "2016 November General Election Turnout Rates," 2016. http://www.electproject.org/2016g.

Wineburg, Sam, Sarah McGrew, Joel Breakstone, and Teresa Ortega. "Evaluating Information: The Cornerstone of Civic Online Reasoning." *Stanford Digital Repository*, Stanford History Education Group, 22 November 2016. https://sheg.stanford.edu/upload/V3LessonPlans /Executive%20Summary%2011.21.16.pdf.

TWO

From Yellow Journalism to Tabloids to Clickbait: The Origins of Fake News in the United States

Sharon McQueen

Scholars may debate the definition and starting point of fake news, but, at its most basic, fake news is a lie. One might, therefore, reasonably surmise that fake news originated with the dawn of human speech.

INTRODUCTION

In the late summer of 1835, as New York City turned its attentions skyward in anticipation of Halley's Comet, the main news page of *The Sun* reported that Sir John Herschel, a renowned British astronomer of the day, had discovered life on the moon—life so strange and marvelous that it almost defied belief ("Great Astronomical Discoveries," 1835). Almost (Copeland 2007, p. 147).

What Sir John Herschel saw—and what *The Sun* exclusively reported— caused a sensation not only in New York but around the country and, indeed, around the world. This was quite an accomplishment for a newspaper that had been in publication for just under two years. It was also quite an accomplishment for Richard Adams Locke, who had been hired as the newspaper's editor only two months prior to the story's publication. In time, the public would come to know that Locke was not only the editor of such stories but their author as well.

Figure 2.1   "Lunar animals and other objects. . . ." (Lithograph issued by *The Sun*, 1835. Courtesy of the Library of Congress [Day 1835])

Locke made sure that if his readers wanted specifics on the wonders of the moon, they would have to buy the next day's paper—and the next. Only after six papers had been purchased did the eager public obtain the full story of the moon's lakes with beaches of "brilliant white sand," forests of trees with "tresses of yellow flowers," and animals that included horned bears, bluish-colored unicorns, bipedal beavers who built huts and had acquired the use of fire, and four-foot-tall humanoid bats (Locke 1835, pp. 11–20). These latter beings, who were observed to have acquired speech, Herschel labeled *Vespertilio-homo*, or man-bat. They were considered to be "innocent and happy creatures, notwithstanding some of their amusements would but ill comport with our terrestrial notions of decorum" (Locke, pp. 20–21). (See Figure 2.1.)

According to Matt Goodman, author of *The Sun and the Moon*, public opinion on the veracity of these scientific reports "was sharply divided, with, by all accounts, a significant majority of New Yorkers leaning toward belief" (Goodman 2008, p. 12).

No other newspaper story of the age was as broadly circulated as Locke's moon series. A pamphlet containing the complete series sold twenty thousand copies in its first week, an exhausting but highly lucrative one for the *Sun*'s newsboys. The articles were reprinted in many of New York's competing newspapers, and later, in newspapers across the country. Illustrated editions were published in Great Britain, Italy, Germany, France. By the time the series had run its course, the *Sun* had become the most widely read newspaper in the world. (Goodman 2008, p. 12)

The stories were read widely by believers and nonbelievers alike. Those who did not take the reports to be true included P. T. Barnum and Edgar Allan Poe. Both men spoke of The Great Moon Hoax, as it came to be called, as a "sensation." In fact, within a few decades, "sensationalism" became known as a style of journalism that selects subject matter and employs a writing style meant to excite and entice the public. A century later, in 1950, Pulitzer Prize–winning historian and journalist Frank Luther Mott listed some of the familiar topics of sensationalism, including crime, scandal, sex, gossip, and pseudo science, along with the use of misleading headlines, faked pictures, faked interviews, and faked stories (Mott 1950, p. 539). Sound familiar?

Many elements of The Great Moon Hoax appear in the fake news stories of our time. For example, the Moon Hoax contained strong elements of truth. Sir John Herschel was a real person, of course, a renowned British astronomer who hailed from a family of astronomers. His father discovered Uranus (no joke), and King George III appointed the elder Herschel to be the first King's Astronomer as a result.[1] In addition, at the time of the articles' printing, Sir John Herschel really was in South Africa, having set up an observatory at the Cape of Good Hope (Goodman 2008, p. 141). *The Edinburgh Journal of Science*, from which *The Sun* claimed to be reprinting reports, was entirely real and prestigious, though it had ceased publishing under that name in 1832.[2]

The authors of fake news stories are often hard, if not impossible to trace. The reports to *The Edinburgh Journal of Science* were submitted by Herschel's amanuensis, Dr. Andrew Grant. No such person existed, and Herschel was difficult to reach for verification. In addition, Locke chose a topic that already held the public's attention (astronomy) and wrote in an official-sounding manner. As is the case with fake news today, in order to be successful, Locke didn't have to get it right, he merely needed to get it just right enough to fool sufficient numbers of people. "Sufficient numbers" will depend upon the goal of each fake news creator, but other elements of fake news have recurred through the ages. As Harvard University historian Robert Darnton has recently written:

> In the long history of misinformation, the current outbreak of fake news has already secured a special place. . . . But the concoction of alternative facts is hardly rare, and the equivalent of today's poisonous, bite-size texts and tweets can be found in most periods of history, going back to the ancients. (Darnton 2017, n.p.)

YELLOW JOURNALISM ANTECEDENTS AND REFORM EFFORTS

Scholars may debate the definition and starting point of fake news, but, at its most basic, fake news is a lie. One might, therefore, reasonably surmise that fake news originated with the dawn of human speech. Certainly, instances of false documents date back to ancient times. For example, in 1275 BCE, the Egyptian pharaoh Rameses II (Rameses the Great) commissioned false accounts of the Battle of Qadesh, one of the most famous battles of the ancient world. Rameses II is depicted as gloriously victorious in these accounts, though Columbia University history professor Marc Van De Mieroop informs us that "most historians regard Rameses's claims of a great victory with some skepticism and argue that the battle was a draw at best" (Van De Mieroop 2011, p. 221). Rameses's motivations may have included personal pride or political gain, but many other historical instances of fake news have had far more dangerous consequences.

In Italy, in 1475 CE, Franciscan friar Bernardine of Feltre (Bernardino da Feltre) delivered several anti-Semitic sermons in which he called for the expulsion of the Jews from Italy and predicted that Jews would murder a Christian child during Passover. When the body of a two-year-old boy named Simon (Simonino) was found in Trent on Easter Sunday, members of three Jewish families were arrested and charged with murder ("Simon of Trent," n.d.). In one of the most atrocious examples of blood libel (i.e., a false accusation of the use of Christian blood in religious rituals), 18 men were tortured, confessions procured, and 15 death sentences issued. The women were placed under house arrest with their children. Under torture, the women denounced their men and converted to Christianity (Po-chia Hsia 1996). One of the condemned men had his flesh torn out by pincers as he was being transported to the execution grounds. Those who requested baptism could avoid being burned at the stake—alive anyway. They were beheaded prior to their bodies being burned (Po-chia Hsia 1996, pp. 67–68).

A few Christian neighbors of the accused attempted in vain to intervene, as did Pope Sixtus IV, but the fever pitch of the popular sentiment ignited and fueled by Bernardine of Feltre made intervention difficult, if not impossible. The story of Simon's "martyrdom" continued to spread, along with additional fake news, and with it more persecution (Po-chia Hsia 1996, pp. 128–129). Simon's cult expanded to numerous communities in northern Italy and southern Germany. A chapel in St. Peter's of Trent was dedicated to Simon, miracles were attributed to him, and he was depicted in "poems, hagiographies, paintings, and other iconographic representations" (Po-chia Hsia 1996, p. 132). It was not until 1965 that the cult of Simon of Trent was abolished by papal decree and Simon was removed from the calendar of saints' days (Po-chia Hsia 1996, p. 135). (See Figure 2.2.)

Figure 2.2 *Der Stürmer*, May 1934. The headline reads, "Jewish Murder Plan against Gentile Humanity Revealed." (Courtesy of Randall Bytwerk's German Propaganda Archive [Opper 1894])

Though we would like to think we are centuries removed from fake news such as this, we are not. Blood libel continued to be used as a justification for anti-Semitism for centuries. In affirmation of just how terrifyingly tenacious fake news can be, articles on the Jewish ritual murder of Christians appeared with some regularity in *Der Stürmer*, a newspaper published in Nazi Germany, and cases of blood libel have been documented into the current century.[3] To this day, even Simon of Trent lives on in online fake news.[4] As historian and MacArthur Fellow Jacob Soll has written, "From the start, fake news has tended to be sensationalist and extreme, designed to inflame passions and prejudices. And it has often provoked violence" (Soll 2016, n.p.).

The Internet and social media platforms are not the first technological developments to have spurred the spread of fake news. Johannes Gutenberg's advances in printing processes during the mid-1400s had many unforeseen consequences, including the wider circulation of fake news in the Western world. Though various printing technologies have existed for thousands of years, and movable type was invented and developed in China by the Chinese printer Bi Sheng between the years 1041 and 1048 CE, Johannes Gutenberg introduced mechanical movable type to Europe. In addition, he made technological improvements that allowed for the mass production of printed materials. With journalistic ethics and standards still hundreds of years in the future, fake news ran rampant. But the history of fake news also contains instances of efforts to thwart it.

The lowly footnote played an important role in providing readers with a means of identifying reliable reports of various kinds. Though British printer Richard Jugge is often given credit for inventing the footnote in 1568, historians are frequently credited for its development. Princeton University historian Anthony Grafton writes:

> Scholars have placed the birth of the footnote in the twelfth century, the seventeenth, the eighteenth, and the nineteenth—never without good reason, but usually without attending to the other chapters in this story. . . . The footnote is not so uniform and reliable as some historians believe. Nor is it the pretentious, authoritarian device that other historians reject. It is the creation of a varied and talented group, one that included philosophers as well as historians. Its development took a long time and followed a bumpy path. (Grafton 1997)[5]

Galileo Galilei, an instrumental figure of the Scientific Revolution, worked to report scientific discovery in such a way that his reader could distinguish between true and fake reports. He advocated for experimentation that was documented and reproducible.[6] He also played a galvanizing role within the European scientific community when he was tried, threatened with torture, and sentenced to imprisonment after publication of his treatise *The Starry Message* (*Sidereus Nuncius*) in 1610.[7] Galileo had spoken of the Copernican system as factual, which set him into conflict with the Catholic Church. Due, at least in part, to the injustices Galileo endured, learned societies and national scientific institutions were formed, scholarly journals were founded, and the peer review process was begun. Reliable, verifiable, scholarly news was the result (Dear 1985; Lipking 2014; Soll 2016, n.p.).

A few centuries later, fake news incensed 18th-century Enlightenment philosopher and historian Voltaire (Grafton 1997, pp. 94–96; Soll 2016, n.p.).[8] On All Saints' Day 1755, the strongest seismic event known to have occurred in Europe nearly destroyed the capital of Portugal and caused considerable damage in other areas of the country (Kozák and Cermák 2010, p. 131). The Great Lisbon Earthquake of 1755, as the event became known, was followed by a tsunami and numerous fires, all of which ruined or heavily damaged 85 percent of the city's houses and killed roughly 20 percent of the population.

Church officials and other European authorities declared that the disaster was the result of God's wrath against sinners. Numerous *relações de sucesso* (i.e., popular fake news pamphlets) appeared in Portugal, "claiming that some survivors owed their lives to an apparition of the Virgin Mary" (Soll 1996, n.p.; Araújo 2006, pp. 1–11).[9] A contentious debate "arose as to whether the earthquake was of natural or supernatural character, with theologians and philosophers on both sides" (Udías 2009, p. 41). Voltaire not only rebelled against supernatural explanations for natural events but used the Great Lisbon Earthquake in his satirical novel *Candide*.

A few years later, Voltaire railed against the fake news that convicted a father of the murder of his eldest son. In 1761, Protestant merchant Jean Calas was rumored to have murdered his son to prevent him from converting to Catholicism. With no hard evidence of murder, rumors and hearsay were turned "into official facts, and, in turn, official news" (Soll 1996, n.p.). Despite gruesome and prolonged public torture, Jean Calas did not confess. Finally he was strangled and his body burned. What famously became known as the Calas affair was not only a turning point in Voltaire's life but a turning point for penal reform in Europe (Davidson 2012, pp. 317–320).

Voltaire fought hard to uncover the facts of the case and to make them widely known. In the end, he realized he was fighting not only for justice for the family of Jean Calas but for judicial system reform—the reform of a system that could use hearsay as evidence. In an even broader sense, Voltaire understood that he was fighting against fanaticism, prejudice, superstition, and fake news. His *Treatise on Tolerance on the Occasion of the Death of Jean Calas from the Judgment Rendered in Toulouse*, published in 1763, was a milestone of the Enlightenment.' In 1765, Jean Calas was posthumously exonerated, and his family was paid 39,000 francs (Davidson 2012, p. 330).

Early efforts such as these impeded the creation, dissemination, and consumption of fake news, but they did not defeat it. Nearly two decades after the publication of Voltaire's *Treatise on Tolerance*, in 1782, cunningly convincing fake news was circulated as peace negotiations began between the United States and Britain following the American Revolutionary War. The culprit? None other than Founding Father Benjamin Franklin—for among his many other accomplishments and titles, Franklin was, after all, a printer.

In preliminary peace negotiation discussions with London merchant Richard Oswald, Franklin suggested a reparations proposal in which Britain would cede control of Canada to the United States. As Franklin biographer Walter Isaacson writes, "The money that America made from selling open land in Canada could be used to compensate the patriots whose homes had been destroyed by British troops and also the British loyalists whose estates had been confiscated by the Americans" (Isaacson 2003, p. 401). Franklin later regretted suggesting compensation to British loyalists but strongly felt that reparations to the patriots were necessary. Believing that a sense of guilt would be useful if it could be instilled in the British public, he set to work at the press he had founded in 1777 at Passy in Paris (Adams 1956, pp. 133–138). Franklin created:

> a fake issue of a Boston newspaper that purported to describe, in gruesome detail, the horrors that the British had perpetrated on innocent Americans. His goal was to emphasize that no sympathy was due the British loyalists, and that it was the Americans who deserved compensation. The fake edition was cleverly convincing. It featured a description of a shipment of American scalps purportedly sent by the Seneca Indians to England and a letter that he pretended was from John Paul Jones. To make it more realistic, he even included fake little ads about a new brick house for sale in south Boston and a missing bay mare in Salem. (Isaacson 2003, p. 402)

Franklin judiciously circulated his fake issue, and some British publications took it to be true, reprinted parts of it, and thus replicated and further distributed the fake news.[10]

Honesty is the best policy.

—Maxim erroneously attributed
to Benjamin Franklin[11]

THE PENNY PRESS, SENSATIONALISM, AND THE RISE OF RELIABLE NEWS

As a young United States progressed into the 1800s, the press was protected by the First Amendment to the United States Constitution, which ensured that Congress could not constrain the freedom of speech or the press. So unconstrained would some New York City newspapers become that boycotts would be organized in attempts to put them out of business.

In 1833, New York City's population numbered more than 250,000, not counting Brooklyn and other nearby municipalities—yet the combined circulation of the City's 11 daily newspapers was only 26,500. (Brooklyn was an independent city until 1898.) At a price of 6¢ apiece, or $10 for an annual subscription, newspapers were too costly for all but the upper classes (Goodman 2008, pp. 20–21). That changed when Benjamin Day published the first edition of *The Sun* on September 3, 1833.

Though Day was only 23 years old, he had worked in the printing trade since the age of 14. Day envisioned a new sort of newspaper, one not meant for merchants, politicians, and the wealthy—but for working people such as himself. Day charged a penny a paper and $3 for a year's subscription, to be paid in advance (Goodman 2008, p. 27).[12] His paper was of a much smaller size than the standard "blanket sheets," which were 3 feet long by 2 feet wide, measuring 4 feet across when opened. Day's paper was a mere 8 by 11 inches, which eliminated the need for the large surfaces on which newspapers were read (Goodman 2008, p. 28). *The Sun* could be read anywhere and almost anytime, as articles tended to be brief. Sometimes more than two dozen filled a page. As Goodman writes, the stories were "often amusing, and strongly seasoned with sex, romance, intrigue, violence, death—the types of stories Benjamin Day figured most New Yorkers wanted to read about." The new daily paper "was—in both meanings of the word—sensational" (Goodman 2008, p. 30).

The trade convention of the day had been to place news stories on page two. Works of fiction, clearly labeled as such, were sometimes placed on the front page. In his first issue, Day ran a front-page story of a Vermont boy so prone to whistling that he even whistled in his sleep, resulting in a "total prostration of strength." Convinced that the condition would end in the boy's death, his mother placed him "in the society of another boy, who had orders to give him a blow as soon as he began to whistle." "A Whistler" appeared on the front page but was formatted as a news story. So what was it—news or fiction? Day did not feel compelled to say ("A Whistler" 1833, p. 1).

New Yorkers did indeed want to read the types of stories Benjamin Day published, but within the first week, Day realized he would either need to hire additional employees or work round the clock. Again his approach broke the mold. Day became the first newspaperman to employ an on-staff court reporter, whose crime stories eventually filled a third of the news page, and he took a chance on a 10-year-old Irish boy named Bernard Flaherty for sales (Goodman 2008, pp. 33–34, 37). Flaherty employed the techniques of the fruit sellers, and other venders who hawked their wares in the streets, by shouting about the newspaper's most tantalizing stories. This practice, which would become known in the newspaper trade as "hollering," was so successful that additional boys were hired to do the same. It was "a new kind of selling for a new kind of newspaper" (Goodman 2008, p. 2).[13] By year's end, *The Sun* was selling thousands of penny papers daily.

The Sun's success quickly spawned imitators. Roughly six months after Day had launched *The Sun*, two of his employees broke off and founded their own penny paper, the *New York Transcript*. The *Transcript* closely followed *The Sun*'s format and content but added more sports, such as boxing and horse racing. As 1834 reached a close, the *Transcript* was closing in on *The Sun*'s circulation figures. In May of 1835, yet another rival penny paper was launched, *Morning Herald* (later *New York Herald*). With the driven Scotsman James Gordon Bennett at the helm, the *Morning Herald* approached *The Sun*'s circulation within two months.

When Benjamin Day lost his editor in May of 1835, he knew he needed an individual who could deal with the ever increasing competition. Richard Adams Locke received the position after writing a sensational series of freelance articles for *The Sun* on the murder trial of Robert Matthews, the self-proclaimed Matthias the Prophet. The "pretended prophet" grew his hair and beard long, dressed in a green robe lined with pink silk, carried a sword, and attracted wealthy New Yorkers to Mount Zion, as he called his communal cult located just north of the City.[14] With adultery, violence, robbery, and a murder charge, Day had the makings of penny paper gold. What he needed was a good storyteller. Richard Adams Locke delivered. The immensely popular five-article series was subsequently gathered and sold in pamphlet form, 6,000 copies of which Day's newsboys dispersed on the first day of release alone (Goodman 2008, p. 75).

Locke's Great Moon Hoax would follow much the same pattern—except that it was not merely sensational news: It was fake.[15] While many other newspapers reprinted Locke's articles of life on the moon, the *Transcript* took things further, running a series of its own entitled "More Lunar

Discoveries, NOT contained in the Supplement to the Edinburgh Journal of Science" (Goodman 2008, p. 205). These were followed by the installments of Baron Hans Phaall, a Dutch astronomer and aeronaut who had traveled to the moon by balloon. Not to be outdone, James Gordon Bennett used the pages of the *Herald* to run an exclusive: "The Astronomical Hoax Explained," in which he was the first to claim that the original moon stories had been made up by Locke. This scoop was "an intoxicating mixture of truth, half-truth, and outright libel" (Goodman 2008, p. 209).

James Gordon Bennett expected *The Sun*'s circulation to plummet after Locke's articles were revealed to be a hoax, but that didn't happen. New Yorkers appeared to view the matter as a first-rate practical joke. Horace Greeley, then editor of the literary weekly *The New Yorker*, was magnanimous about having been taken in by the hoax and praised Locke's ingenuity. Even Bennett had referred to Locke as a genius and had glowingly praised his literary abilities. Such praise was highly unusual from a man who frequently wrote scathing editorials about competing New York editors. Clearly, there was very little to lose in printing fake news, and the financial gains had proven to be enormous.

Richard Adams Locke was a rarity among New York City editors: He had few enemies. Locke generally stayed above the fray of the fierce rivalry among newspaper editors, rivalry with such bitter personal resentments that acrimonious verbal encounters often became physical. Famed poet, abolitionist, and editor of the *New York Evening Post* William Cullen Bryant once engaged in a public exchange of editorial insults with William Leete Stone, editor of the *Commercial Advertiser*. Bryant horsewhipped Stone in the streets of New York, and Stone retaliated by striking back with a bamboo cane "that shattered on impact, revealing inside it a long, slender steel sword" (Goodman 2008, p. 20). In 1836, the editor of the *Courier and Enquirer* struck James Gordon Bennett three times within the span of a few weeks. For his part, Bennett kept a set of loaded pistols in his office as defense against his enemies. And they were many. In fact, in "an industry dominated by arrogant, egotistical men, Bennett was the *ne plus ultra* [the ultimate example]" (Goodman 2008, p. 20). As one contemporary newspaper editor put it, Bennett was:

> A reptile marking his path with slime wherever he goes, and breathing mildew at every thing fresh and fragrant; a midnight ghoul, preying on rottenness and repulsive filth; a creature, hated by his nearest intimates, and bearing the consciousness thereof upon his distorted

features, and upon his despicable soul; one whom good men avoid as a blot to his nature—whom all despise, and whom no one blesses— all this is James Gordon Bennett. (Whitman 1842, p. 2)

The author of this diatribe was none other than Walt Whitman, who was the editor of the *New York Aurora* at the time.[16]

Bennett not only survived the written attacks of other editors, but he also survived a duel, an assassination attempt, and a boycott designed to put the *Herald* out of business (Goodman 2008, pp. 83–84). New York's newspapers put aside their differences to join in the concerted effort, which became known as the Moral War (Birdsong 1925, pp. 41–42, 70). Though it was a war the moralists did not win, it did play a role in Horace Greeley's decision to found the *New-York Tribune* in 1841. Greeley would make a great success of a newspaper "with a moral agenda and an interest in improving society" (Long 1998, p. 31). As historian and journalist Allan Nevins explained, the "*Tribune* set a new standard in American journalism by its combination of energy in news gathering with good taste, high moral standards, and intellectual appeal. . . . The paper appealed to substantial and thoughtful people" (Nevins 1935, p. 12).

When the first issue of the *New-York Tribune* was released, Bennett's *Herald* enjoyed a larger circulation than all of New York City's newspapers combined (Williams 2006, p. 57). By 1860, Greeley's *Tribune* enjoyed a larger circulation than any newspaper in the world, proving that there was a market for reliable news (Williams 2006, p. 1). Greeley's success was so great that, as had been the case with editors before him, one of Greeley's employees endeavored to establish a newspaper of his own—a daily paper that would "avoid sensationalism and report the news in a restrained and objective fashion" ("*The New York Times*" 2017, n.p.). So in 1851, a new penny paper hit the scene: *The New York Times*.[17]

YELLOW JOURNALISM AND THE RISE OF STANDARDS AND ETHICS

Despite the new beginning for reliable journalism in the mid-1800s, sensationalism and fake news continued to sell papers. And despite the fact that the market for newspapers continued to expand at a phenomenal rate, competition for readers remained fierce.[18] The best known of the circulation battles took place between Joseph Pulitzer's *The New York World* and William Randolph Hearst's *New York Journal*.

Pulitzer and Hearst both had extensive regional newspaper experience when they entered the New York City newspaper world: Pulitzer in St. Louis, Missouri, Hearst in San Francisco. Both were well educated and wealthy, and both chose to purchase fiscally troubled New York newspapers. Pulitzer purchased *The New York World* from Jay Gould in 1883, and Hearst bought the *Journal* in 1895.

Gould had purchased *The World* from "a group headed by Thomas A. Scott, president of the Pennsylvania Railroad. . . . who bought it as a propaganda vehicle for his own stock enterprises" (Swanberg 1967, p. 67). Gould, in turn, used *The World* to advance his own agenda. Though Gould's use of *The World* aided him in his effort to gain control of Western Union, as one of the well-known "robber barons" of the Gilded Age, he was unable to sell enough papers to a public that despised him (Swanberg 1967, p. 67). *The World* continued to operate in the red, and Gould put the paper up for sale.

Joseph Pulitzer was ready to take on the challenge of building circulation and turning losses into profits. By the time he purchased *The World*, sensationalism was being employed by various newspapers from coast to coast. Headlines grabbed readers' attention with large type, all caps, hyperbole, and alliteration (Bulla and Sachsman 2013, p. xxi). The *Chicago Times*, for example, drew attention to the execution of a convicted murderer in 1875 with the headline "JERKED TO JESUS!" ("JERKED TO JESUS!" 1875). Though Pulitzer was a social reformer and intellectual at heart—and his journalistic practices reflected this—he was also fully willing to engage in the worst excesses of the day, and then some. (See Figure 2.3.)

Pulitzer was not afraid to experiment and innovate. He began using a four-color printing press and was an early adopter of the color supplement. *The World's* Sunday supplement was one of the first to feature comic strips, the premier issue of which contained Richard F. Outcault's highly popular strip, *Hogan's Alley*. One character, Mickey Dugan, was a young street urchin dressed in an oversized nightshirt. Once color became an option, and yellow was selected for Dugan's nightshirt, the character became known as "The Yellow Kid." (See Figure 2.4.)

By the time the 32-year-old William Randolph Hearst arrived in New York in 1895, the "dominant publishers of the previous decade were ailing, or absent, or both" (Campbell 2015, p. 3). Pulitzer, no longer a young man, was going blind. He spent most of his time outside the City, managing matters primarily by telegram (Campbell 2015, p. 6). He made no secret of the fact that he intended to engage in a circulation war not only with

Figure 2.3   In this 1894 illustration, a reporter rushes to bring fake news to the newspaper's proprietor, who is getting rich as a result. Though the newspaper is labeled the *Daily Splurge*, its proprietor bears a striking resemblance to Joseph Pulitzer. (Courtesy of the Library of Congress [Opper 1894])

Pulitzer but with all the other editors of papers that had once been known as "the penny press," including James Gordon Bennett, Jr., who had taken the helm of the *New York Herald*.

Though other papers had raised their price to 2¢, Hearst decided to offer the "*Journal* at a penny, but give readers as much news, entertainment, sports, and spectacle as Joseph Pulitzer's *World*, Bennett's *Herald*, and

Figure 2.4 Poster advertising the August 16, 1896, *New York World* issue featuring "The Yellow Kid" from "Hogan's Alley," by Richard F. Outcault. Note the sensationalized headlines including, "BABIES USED as Bait for MONSTERS." (Courtesy of the Library of Congress)

Dana's *Sun* provided for twice that price" (Nasaw 2000, p. 100). Hearst's advertisement and promotion of the *Journal* was extravagant. He hired staff who could assure that the *Journal*'s writing and illustrations were unmatched—even if he had to lure them from rival papers to do it (Nasaw 2000, p. 102).

In October of 1896, Hearst induced Richard F. Outcault to leave Pulitzer's employ and acquired The Yellow Kid as a result. Though Pulitzer held the copyright to *Hogan's Alley*, Outcault was legally free to use his characters in a new strip, entitled *McFadden's Row of Flats*. Pulitzer simply replaced Outcault with George Luks, and *Hogan's Alley* lived on. The rival publishers now both had rival Yellow Kids.

Hearst began referring to his endeavors as the "new journalism," and he began depicting his competitors, sometimes in humorous illustrations, as relics of a previous era. His competitors fought back. Ervin Wardman, editor of the *New York Press*, was "a fastidious man who resented and deplored the bold and aggressive journalism of Hearst and, to a lesser extent, Joseph Pulitzer" (Campbell 2015, p. 5). Wardman first attempted a play on "new journalism," asking "Why not call it nude journalism?" (Campbell 2001b, p. 32). After all, Wardman believed, such journalism had not "even the veneer of decency" (Campbell 2001b, p. 32). But in January of 1897, Wardman lit upon a term that would clearly encompass both Hearst and Pulitzer: "yellow-kid journalism," which was shortened eight days later to "yellow journalism" (Campbell 2001b, p. 32). The epithet has been with us ever since. (See Figure 2.5.)

As the editorial cartoon by Barritt (1898) illustrates, Hearst and yellow journalism have been credited with inciting, among other events, the Spanish-American War. One of the best known anecdotes in American journalism involves telegrams supposedly sent between Hearst and artist Frederic Remington. Remington and reporter Richard Harding Davis were sent to Cuba to cover the revolt for Cuban independence from Spain in January of 1897. Remington purportedly cabled, "Everything is quiet. There will be no war. I wish to return." Hearst is said to have responded, "Please remain. You furnish the pictures, and I'll furnish the war." Recent scholarship, most notably by historian W. Joseph Campbell, argues that this exchange was unlikely to have occurred.[19]

Campbell insists that "the mythology and misunderstanding that embrace Hearst and yellow journalism are probably too delicious, too ingrained, and too often repeated ever to be fully corrected" (Campbell 2015, p. 13). He further points out that "there was more than flash, frivolity, and bold

Figure 2.5 Lithograph depicting Joseph Pulitzer and William Randolph Hearst as "The Yellow Kid." (Courtesy of the Library of Congress [Barritt 1898])

headlines to Hearst's journalism. Much more." (Campbell 2015, p. 7). Nevertheless, critics of the excesses of yellow journalism, both in its heyday and in retrospect, have been many.

By 1898, a newspaper trade publication noted, "The public is becoming heartily sick of fake news and fake extras. Some of the newspapers in this town have printed so many lying dispatches that people are beginning to mistrust any statement they make" (Pomerantz 1958, 59). Historian Sidney I. Pomerantz argues that by the turn of the century, "yellow journalism was on the decline, with [Pulitzer's] the *World* leading the way back to 'normalcy'" (Pomerantz 1958, p. 60). Pomerantz also credits the rise of *The New York Times* for the shift.

But, as digital researcher and writer Alexandra Samuel points out, "to say that yellow journalism waned because the public wanted something better is to oversimplify the story" (Samuel 2016, n.p.). In addition to a shift toward a public desire for reliable news in the late 19th century, there was a shift in the U.S. courts' attitudes toward the media and its "intrusions into the lives of public figures" (Samuel 2016, n.p.). Media law scholar Amy Gajda notes that today's concept of our right to privacy can be traced to "the prying eyes of yellow journalists and gossip-mongers" (Gajda 2009, p. 1045). In the early decades of the 20th century, Gajda observes that "the weight of decisions during this period held newspapers and other related media responsible for privacy invasions with growing frequency" (Gajda 2009, pp. 1048–1049).

The newspaper industry itself also played a substantial role in reform. As early as 1892, Joseph Pulitzer had offered to fund the world's first school of journalism at Columbia University. Though he was initially turned down, Pulitzer had made provisions for the school in his will. The Columbia University Graduate School of Journalism was funded in 1912.[20] The Pulitzer Prizes in journalism were established at Columbia in 1917 ("History of the Pulitzer Prizes" 2018, n.p.).

The Kansas State Editorial Association adopted the industry's first code of ethics in 1910, which condemned fake illustrations, fake interviews, and fake news dispatches ("Code of Ethics" 1922). During the following decades, similar codes were adopted throughout the United States. By 1955, the *American Bar Association Journal* contained the following pronouncement: "In recent decades the press of the nation has developed a code of ethics to which it adheres within reason, though sometimes stooping a little to get results" (Cullinan 1955, pp. 1063–1064).

Clearly, major gains had been made. And yet, in that same decade, a tiny spider could make a wry comment that rang true—a comment that caused us to smile but at the same time caused us to stop and ponder our own gullibility.

"But Charlotte," said Wilbur, "I'm not terrific."

"That doesn't make a particle of difference," replied Charlotte. "Not a particle. People believe almost anything they see in print. Does anybody here know how to spell 'terrific'?"

—E.B. White, *Charlotte's Web*, 1952

CONCLUSION: WHY THE HISTORY OF FAKE NEWS MATTERS

As yellow journalism receded, tabloids arose in the 1920s and 1930s, beginning with the *Daily News* in 1919.[21] These daily publications morphed into the weekly supermarket tabloids of today, which never gained mainstream credibility. Though often mean-spirited, supermarket tabloids have generally been viewed as harmless and jejune over the course of their history. The same cannot be said of much of today's fake news.

History has demonstrated that people will use various platforms as fake news vehicles for their own personal gain. These gains—whether they be financial, political, or social—can be enormous. As history has also demonstrated, fake news can be dangerous. It can enable the oppression of and even violence against individuals and groups. Jacob Soll ends his article "The Long and Brutal History of Fake News" by cautioning us that "as real news recedes, fake news will grow. We've seen the terrifying results this has had in the past—and our biggest challenge will be to find a new way to combat the rising tide" (Soll 2016, n.p.).

The Calas affair and the injustices suffered by Galileo were influential catalysts in Enlightenment battles against fake news. Yellow journalism was the catalyst for the development of journalistic standards and ethics. What will today's society do to combat clickbait?

Like Voltaire, we have a fight on our hands. In the 1760s, Voltaire fully understood that he was fighting against fanaticism, prejudice, superstition, and fake news. Do we understand this today? If so, we must develop and employ tools that can assist us in the fight. The book you now hold in your hands is one such tool.

Beware of stories you want to be true, for whatever reason.[22]

—Ben Bradlee, American newspaperman (1995)

NOTES

1. Sir John Herschel's aunt, Caroline Herschel, was also a highly regarded astronomer.

2. *The Edinburgh Journal of Science* was published under that title from 1824 to 1832 and was succeeded by *The London and Edinburgh Philosophical Magazine and Journal of Science* and *Philosophical Magazine*.

3. See, for example, "Jews Accused in the Murder of Krasnoyarsk Children," *Regnum*, May 12, 2005. https://regnum.ru/news/454284.html.

4. See, for example, Mark Downey, "Jewish Ritual Murder," Kinsman Redeemer Ministries. http://kinsmanredeemer.com/jewish-ritual-murder.

5. For more on Richard Jugge and the footnote, see Chuck Zerby, *The Devil's Details: A History of Footnotes* (New York: Touchstone [Simon & Schuster], 2003), pp. 19–39.

6. "'There was no such thing as the Scientific Revolution,' Steven Shapin's popular survey begins, 'and this is a book about it.' A paradox and a commonplace meet in that sentence. For more than two decades, historians of science have been expressing misgivings about 'the Scientific Revolution' as a phrase and a 'thing.' Yet a great many of them continue to write about it." Lipking, *What Galileo Saw: Imagining the Scientific Revolution* (Ithaca, NY: Cornell University Press, 2014), p. 210.

7. Galileo's sentence was commuted to house arrest. He remained under house arrest for the rest of his life.

8. Voltaire was the nom de plume of François-Marie Arouet.

9. For an example of a widely distributed attribution of God's wrath as the earthquake's cause, see John Wesley, *Serious Thoughts Occasioned by the late Earthquake at Lisbon* (London: Bristol, 1755).

10. The September 27, 1782 issue of *Public Advertiser* states that (the faked) John Paul Jones letter will appear the following day, which it does (*Public Advertiser*, September 27, 1782, 1–2). Much of Franklin's work, attributed to his *Boston Independent Chronicle*, appeared in *The Remembrancer; or Impartial Repository of Public Events for 1782*, Part II, Volume 14, London: J. Debrett, 135–136 (https://archive.org/stream/TheReme mbrancerOrImpartialRepositoryOfPublicEventsvol.14/Almon-TheReme mbrancer1782PartIi#page/n5/mode/2up). Franklin admitted the fake nature of his "news" to John Adams in 1782. For example, Franklin refers to "Paul Jones's pretended letter." Carla J. Mulford, *Benjamin Franklin and the Ends of Empire* (New York: Oxford University Press, 2015), p. 301.

11. "Franklin did cite the maxim 'Honesty is the best policy' in a letter to Edward Bridgen, Oct. 2, 1779, but it was part of a list of maxims that could be on coins. He did not claim it as his own" (Isaacson 2003, p. 561).

12. Benjamin Day was not the first newspaperman to charge a penny per paper. The *Morning Post* had been founded in New York City early that year, in January 1833. The price was initially 2¢, and though the price was quickly dropped to a penny, it was too late to make a difference. Before the end of the month, it had closed. A semiweekly penny paper was published in Boston as the *Boston Evening Bulletin* for little more than a year (December 3, 1827, to December 29, 1828), then as the *Boston Evening Bulletin, and United States Republican* until April 29, 1830. When it ceased publication, publishers saw an opening for a daily penny paper, and *The Boston Transcript* was founded. It was published for over 100 years. Joseph Edgar Chamberlin, *The Boston Transcript: A History of Its First Hundred Years* (Boston: Houghton Mifflin, 1930).

13. For an example of the use of the term "hollering," see William Jay Gaynor, "Hollering," in *Some of Mayor Gaynor's Letters and Speeches* (New York: Greaves, 1913), p. 42.

14. One member of Robert Matthews's cult was a former slave named Isabella Van Wagenen, who would later change her name to Sojourner Truth. Paul E. Johnson and Sean Wilentz, *The Kingdom of Matthias: A Story of Sex and Salvation in 19th-Century America*, 2nd ed. (London: Oxford University Press, 2012).

15. Goodman makes the case that Locke's Great Moon Hoax "had not been intended as a hoax at all; it had been intended as a satire" (Goodman 2008, pp. 277–280).

16. Whitman was responding to a Charles Dickens critic who felt that Dickens's evil characters were exaggerated, as there are "no such creatures in the world, or in nature." While only 23 years of age at the time, Walt Whitman had seen enough of yellow journalism that he begged to differ, stating that "there is a palpable counterpart to the worst embodiment of evil that the brain of Dickens ever transcribed upon paper!" That "palpable counterpart" was James Gordon Bennett.

17. *The New York Times* was founded as the *New-York Daily Times* in 1851. The daily penny paper was rebranded *The New-York Times* in 1857. The hyphen was dropped in 1896.

18. In 1833, there were roughly 1,200 newspapers in the United States. By 1860, that number had more than doubled. By 1870, there were approximately 4,500, and by 1890, about 12,000. The increased demand for

newspapers was due, in large part, to waves of immigration, increases in urban populations, high literacy rates, and the expansion of advertising (Sachsman 2015, pp. xviii–xix).

19. See for example, Campbell (2001a). For an argument against yellow journalism and its profit motive as the instigator of the Spanish-American War, see, for example, Pérez (1989).

20. The University of Missouri had founded the Missouri School of Journalism in 1908, and the Ecole Supérieure de Journalisme de Paris had been established in 1899.

21. The *Daily News* is still in operation. As was the case with Pulitzer's *World* and Hearst's *Journal*, the *Daily News* has a reputation for "speaking to and for the city's working class," as well as for its "crusades against municipal misconduct" (Feuer 2015, n.p.).

22. Ben Bradlee was the executive editor of *The Washington Post* 1968–1991.

REFERENCES

Adams, Jr., F. B. "Franklin and His Press at Passy." *The Yale University Library Gazette* 30, no. 4 (April 1956): 133–138.

Araújo, Ana Cristina. "The Lisbon Earthquake of 1755—Public Distress and Political Propaganda." *e-JPH (e-Journal of Portuguese History)* 4, no. 1 (Summer 2006): 1–11.

Barritt, Leon, artist. *Vim*, 1, no. 2 (June 29, 1898). Library of Congress Prints and Photographs Division Washington, D.C. 20540. AP101.V55 1898 (Case X) [P&P].

Birdsong, Henry Ellis. *James Gordon Bennett and the New York Herald*. PhM Thesis, University of Wisconsin–Madison, 1925.

Bradlee, Ben. *A Good Life: Newspapering and Other Adventures*. New York: Simon & Schuster, 2017 [reissue c. 1995].

Bulla, David W., and David B. Sachsman (eds.). "Introduction." In *Sensationalism: Murder, Mayhem, Mudslinging, Scandals, and Disasters in 19th-Century Reporting*. New Brunswick, NJ: Transaction Publishers, 2013.

Campbell, W. Joseph. "Not Likely Sent: The Remington–Hearst 'Telegrams.'" In *Yellow Journalism: Puncturing the Myths, Defining the Legacies*, 71–95. Westport, CT: Praeger, 2001a.

Campbell, W. Joseph. *Yellow Journalism: Puncturing the Myths, Defining the Legacies*. Westport, CT: Praeger, 2001b.

Campbell, W. Joseph. "Yellow Journalism: Why So Maligned and Misunderstood?" In David B. Sachsman (ed.), *Sensationalism: Murder, Mayhem, Mudslinging, Scandals, and Disasters in 19th-Century Reporting*, 3–18. New York: Routledge, 2015.

"Code of Ethics for Newspapers Proposed by W. E. Miller of the St. Mary's Star and Adopted by the Kansas State Editorial Association at the State Convention of the Kansas Editorial Association, March 8, 1910." *The Ethics of the Professions and of Business*, in *The Annals of the American Academy of Political and Social Science* 101 (May 1922): 286–294.

Copeland, David A. "A Series of Fortunate Events: Why People Believed Richard Adams Locke's 'Moon Hoax.'" *Journalism History*, 33, no. 3 (Fall 2007): 140–150.

Cullinan, Eustace. "The Rights of Newspapers: May They Print Whatever They Choose?" *American Bar Association Journal* 41, no. 11 (November 1955): 1020–1023, 1063–1064.

Darnton, Robert, "The True Story of Fake News." *The New York Review of Books*, February 13, 2017. http://www.nybooks.com/daily/2017/02/13/the-true-history-of-fake-news.

Davidson, Ian. *Voltaire: A Life*. New York: Pegasus, 2012.

Day, Benjamin Henry, copyright claimant. "Lunar animals and other objects Discovered by Sir John Herschel in his observatory at the Cape of Good Hope and copied from sketches in *The Edinburgh Journal of Science*, 1835." Photograph. https://www.loc.gov/item/2003665049/.

Dear, Peter. "Totius in Verba: Rhetoric and Authority in the Early Royal Society." *Isis* 76, no. 2 (June 1985): 144–161.

Feuer, Alan. "The *Daily News* Layoffs and Digital Shift May Signal the Tabloid Era's End." *The New York Times*, September 27, 2015. https://www.nytimes.com/2015/09/28/nyregion/the-daily-news-layoffs-and-digital-shift-may-signal-the-tabloid-eras-end.html.

Gajda, Amy. "Judging Journalism: The Turn toward Privacy and Judicial Regulation of the Press." *California Law Review* 97, no. 4 (August 2009): 1039–1105.

Goodman, Matt. *The Sun and the Moon: The Remarkable True Account of Hoaxers, Showmen, Dueling Journalists, and Lunar Man-Bats in Nineteenth-Century New York* New York: Basic Books, 2008.

Grafton, Anthony. *The Footnote: A Curious History*, rev. ed., Cambridge, MA: Harvard University Press, 1997.

"Great Astronomical Discoveries, Lately Made by Sir John Herschel, L.L.D.F.R.S. &c. At the Cape of Good Hope [From Supplement to the Edinburgh Journal of Science]," *The Sun*, August 25, 1835, p. 2.

"History of the Pulitzer Prizes." The Pulitzer Prizes, 2018. http://www .pulitzer.org/page/history-pulitzer-prizes.

Isaacson, Walter. *Benjamin Franklin: An American Life*. New York: Simon & Schuster, 2003.

"JERKED TO JESUS!" *Chicago Times*, November 27, 1875.

Kozák, Jan, and Vladimir Cermák. "Great Lisbon Earthquake of 1755." *The Illustrated History of Natural Disasters*. London: Springer, 2010.

Locke, Richard Adams. *Great Astronomical Discoveries, Lately Made by Sir John Herschel, L.L.D.F.R.S. &c. At the Cape of Good Hope* [pamphlet]. New York: *The Sun*, 1835.

Long, Kathryn Teresa. *The Revival of 1857–58: Interpreting an American Religious Awakening*. New York: Oxford University Press, 1998.

Mott, Frank Luther. *American Journalism: A History of Newspapers in the United States through 260 years, 1690 to 1950*. New York: Macmillan, 1950.

Nasaw, David. *The Chief: The Life of William Randolph Hearst*. Boston: Houghton Mifflin, 2000.

Nevins, Allan. "Horace Greeley." In *Dictionary of American Biography*. New York: Scribner's Sons, 1935.

"*The New York Times*: American Newspaper." In *Encyclopaedia Britannica*, 2017. https://www.britannica.com/topic/The-New-York-Times.

Opper, Frederick Burr, artist. "The Fin de Siècle Newspaper Proprietor." *Puck*, March 7, 1894, 35, no. 887. New York: Keppler & Schwarzmann. Library of Congress Prints and Photographs Division. AP101. P7 1894 (Case X) [P&P]. https://www.loc.gov/item/2012648704/.

Pérez, Louis A. "The Meaning of the Maine: Causation and Historiography of the Spanish-American War." *Pacific Historical Review* 58, no. 3 (August 1989): 293–322.

Po-chia Hsia, R. *Trent 1475: Stories of a Ritual Murder Trial*. New Haven, CT: Yale University Press, 1996.

Pomerantz, Sidney. "The Press of a Greater New York: 1898–1900." *New York History* 39, no. 1 (January 1958): 50–66.

Sachsman, David B. *Sensationalism: Murder, Mayhem, Mudslinging, Scandals, and Disasters in 19th-Century Reporting*. New York: Routledge, 2015.

Samuel, Alexandra. "To Fix Fake News, Look to Yellow Journalism." *Jstor Daily*, November 29, 2016. https://daily.jstor.org/to-fix-fake-news -look-to-yellow-journalism.

"Simon of Trent." The Francis A. Countway Library of Medicine: An Alliance of the Boston Medical Library and Harvard Medical School. http://collections.countway.harvard.edu/onview/exhibits/show /sages—scholars—and-healers—/hyams-collection/jewish-life /simon-of-trent.

Soll, Jacob. "The Long and Brutal History of Fake News." *Politico*, December 18, 2016. https://www.politico.com/magazine/story/2016/12/fake -news-history-long-violent-214535.

Swanberg, W. A. *Pulitzer*. New York: Charles A. Scribner & Sons, 1967.

Udías, Agustín. "Earthquakes as God's Punishment in 17th- and 18th-Century Spain." In *Geology and Religion: A History of Harmony and Hostility*, 41–48. London: Geological Society, 2009.

Van De Mieroop, Marc. *History of Ancient Egypt*. Oxford: Wiley-Blackwell, 2011.

"A Whistler," *The Sun*, September 3, 1833, p. 1.

White, E. B. *Charlotte's Web*. New York: Harper & Row, 1952.

Whitman, Walt. "Dickens and Democracy," *New York Aurora*, April 2, 1842, p. 2. The Walt Whitman Archive. https://whitmanarchive.org /published/periodical/journalism/tei/per.00389.html.

Williams, Robert C. *Horace Greeley: Champion of American Freedom*. New York: New York University Press, 2006.

THREE

Critical Literacy as an Approach to Combating Cultural Misinformation/ Disinformation on the Internet*

Nicole A. Cooke

It is easy to get caught up in the hype and excitement of a juicy piece of gossip or in the saccharine mindlessness of YouTube videos featuring babies and pets. Unfortunately, there is another, darker side to this information coin—the inordinate amount of online information that is malicious and damaging.

INTRODUCTION

The Internet is inundated with information of all kinds, and so much of that information is of low to no quality. Yet with lightning speed, a great deal of this information goes viral without being vetted or confirmed. It is easy to get caught up in the hype and excitement of a juicy piece of gossip or in the saccharine mindlessness of YouTube videos featuring babies and pets.

---

* Note: Portions of this chapter are based on ©2017 Nicole A. Cooke, "Posttruth, Truthiness, and Alternative Facts: Information Behavior and Critical Information Consumption for a New Age," *The Library Quarterly* 87, no. 3 (July 2017): 211–221.

Unfortunately, there is another, darker side to this information coin: the inordinate amount of online information that is malicious and damaging. If such information is ever retracted, disproved, or corrected, the damage has been done, and the evidence remains digitally archived.

In conjunction with the potentially damaging misinformation and disinformation is the assumption that Internet users are savvy researchers and intelligent consumers of information because they are adept with technological tools. Abercrombie and Longhurst (1998) refer to this as participation in "mediascapes": Internet users are well-versed in the mechanics of playing games, Photoshopping, creating memes and mashups, and so on but are not discerning with respect to the information that is manipulated and presented to them. Information on the Internet is often viewed as objective and universal, without the understanding that the technology reflects a culture of whiteness and sensibilities that are distinctly Western, masculine, and homogeneous in regard to notions of religion, progress, and modernity. Dinerstein refers to this understanding as the "technocultural matrix" (Dinerstein 2006, p. 571). This particular lens can be particularly inhospitable to messages and content related to any culture located outside of this matrix.

In an age where tweets and Facebook statuses are being reported as news, Internet users need to be competent and intelligent users of information to the point of becoming culture jammers who critique popular culture in an effort to challenge the status quo and resist dominant cultural practices (Lasn 1999; Harris 2004; Carducci 2006; Sandlin 2007; Sandlin and Milam 2008). An approach to reaching this level of critical media consumption is to impart literacy skills to Internet users. Specifically, critical information literacy (Eisenberg, Lowe, and Spitzer 2004; Elmborg, 2006), digital literacy (Bawden and Robinson 2002; Bawden 2008), and cultural competence/literacy (Ladson-Billings 1995; Overall 2009) would facilitate Internet users' ability to seek, find, and use appropriate information, which in turn would facilitate more thoughtful dialogues and learning. Literacy skills would facilitate a shift from rote crowdsourcing of information on the Internet to substance-based evaluation and usage of information.

Electronic information will continue to increase and dominate our society, coloring how we learn, play, and interact with the world. The more information we have access to, the harder it becomes to pick out the good bits, use them, and relevantly apply them to our lives. Devising ways to educate Internet users of all ages, inside and outside formal educational settings, is an important topic not limited to any one area or group of people or to any one discipline of study. The acquisition and implementation of literacy skills is a long-term and integral part of addressing the aforementioned issues.

MISINFORMATION/DISINFORMATION

The concepts of misinformation and disinformation (mis/dis) are discussed specifically in the field of information science (and also in psychology, philosophy, and computer science) and can be thought of as two sides of the same coin. *Misinformation* is simply defined as information that is incomplete (Fox 1983; Losee 1997; Zhou and Zhang 2007), but it can also be categorized as information that is uncertain, vague, or ambiguous. However, misinformation may still be "true, accurate, and informative depending on the context" (Karlova and Lee 2011, p. 3). The *Oxford English Dictionary* defines *disinformation* as "the dissemination of deliberately false information" (http://www.oed.com), particularly when the information is poised to be widely and/or swiftly disseminated, such as information on the Internet (Fallis 2009, p. 3). Fallis (2009) gives more depth and breadth to the definition by suggesting that disinformation is carefully planned, can come from individuals or groups, can be disseminated by entities other than the originators (i.e., misinformation spread by a news organization), and is typically written or verbal information (pp. 1–3). Hernon (1995) concurs by stating "we can put quotation marks around anything and change meaning" and goes on to say that mis/dis is so easily spread because "the person doing the misuse might only be guilty of taking something publicly available, through a listserv or electronic journal or newsletter, without checking the original source" (p. 136).

The key to disinformation is that it is considered borne of maliciousness or ill intent. The scientific community goes as far as to talk about disinformation as the "cultural production of ignorance" and, instead of using the term "disinformation," to coin it *agnotology* (Proctor and Schiebinger 2008, p. 1). However, others argue that disinformation can be motivated by benevolence (i.e., little white lies meant to spare hurt feelings or lying about a surprise) (Walcyz, Runco, Tripp, and Smith 2008; Rubin 2010). In these cases, context helps receivers of the information begin to make sense of the mis/dis (or information in general) being presented to them. Information is valid only if there is a mutual meaning and/or domain knowledge between the sender and receiver of the information. For example, if a person sees a picture of Halloween costumes depicting blackface and has no meaning or understanding of the historical and racial implications, he or she may not be offended by the image or understand why someone else would be upset or angry by that visual.

Because mis/dis is related to discussions and studies of credibility, trustworthiness, and deception, it is often hard to discern the motivations behind this erroneous information sharing. This is especially hard to discern in the online environment where there is an abundance of information (both accurate and inaccurate) and often a lack of visual and aural cues, cues that in real life might alert a consumer of information that something was amiss or false. Because of the pervasiveness of technology in today's world, it is especially important to be cognizant of mis/dis not only because it prohibits collective knowledge and understanding but also because it can indeed do harm by deliberately and persistently perpetuating racist and culturally insensitive images and messages. Zhou and Zhang (2007) state that "with the growing use of the Internet and ubiquitous information access, misinformation is pervasive on the Internet and disseminated though online communication media, which could lead to serious consequences for individuals, organizations, and/or the entire society at large" (p. 804).

THE FALSE ILLUSION OF INTERNET SAVVY

Mediascapes

Abercrombie and Longhurst (1998) suggest that participation in mediascapes is the active use of technology by young adults in an effort to communicate, interact, and be seen by peers. Lankshear and Knobel (2011) continue this argument by detailing how teens make use of digital tools and media, tools that permit instant gratification and allow them to receive attention. What these authors discuss is applicable to the use of social media and digital technology by users of any age. The creation of memes, mashups, and Photoshopped images are more about their producers and their "surface images, style, and brands associated with markers of identity and status" than they are about the content and subjects contained within these digital products (Abercrombie and Longhurst 1998, p. 82). Frequently, mediascapes involve celebrities or other public figures, images, and personalities "that are often confused with the realities" and worlds of the people creating those digital products (Lankshear and Knobel 2011, p. 14).

Mediascapes + Mis/Dis + Cultural Images

Dinerstein's notion (2006) of the technocultural matrix dovetails and extends the discussion of online mis/dis by providing a way to understand why messages and images that fall outside the norms of acceptability and respectability (i.e., things not identified as white, affluent, masculine, modern, etc.) are so readily dismissed and ridiculed or so easily classified as "less-than," exotic, "other," or simply a joke (p. 571). Even when images and messages contain racist or culturally insensitive depictions and implications, they are effortlessly discarded and deemed as not serious, hurtful, or worthy of concern or offense. With this in mind, it becomes clearer how images and messages featuring women and minorities are fetishized, made the butts of jokes and body shaming, and generally made to represent the bad, wrong, and/or evil in society. Images are also routinely and purposely used to perpetuate and exacerbate existing stereotypes.

Carey (1989) suggested that technologies are representations of the culture in which they exist, and as such they cannot be viewed or accepted as neutral or free of biases. Nakamura (2006) picks up this argument by suggesting that the same thing applies to objects and messages on the Internet: They are manifestations of the larger culture and need to be examined and critiqued in a critical and cultural way. Internet messages are part of a "contemporary constellation of racism, globalization, and technoculture" and should be viewed as such (p. 30). Brock (2009) extends this further by stating that cultural images, online texts, and the electronic media that house them are products of the overall culture and society and should even be viewed as potential vehicles of race, power, and discrimination.

Parsing (Cultural) Electronic Images and Messages

Inaccurate information might result from either a deliberate attempt to deceive or mislead (disinformation) or from an honest mistake (misinformation). Either way, incorrect information gets out. Clearly, authenticating and verifying the integrity of a document is more than simply obtaining and using a copy of it. (Hernon 1995, p. 134)

The Internet contains "electronic bandits and other hazards" that eagerly misconstrue messages and images in an attempt to "subvert the certainty of photographic evidence" (Wallich and Mitchell, as cited in Hernon 1995, p. 134). This subversion is prevalent in today's Internet culture and is particularly acute when it comes to cultural messages and images. Per Dinerstein's matrix, messages depicting people of color are especially prone to manipulation and misinterpretation. It is possible that it becomes easier for people to subvert and/or blindly receive altered images and messages because many people lack the understanding of the cultural message in question. Another explanation is that those engaging in mis/dis are making prejudicial assumptions and proving the technocultural matrix to be true. Because receivers of information are themselves not culturally, information, or media literate (to be discussed shortly), they are more apt to passively accept the erroneous information so readily available. An altered or misconstrued image or message has to be outrageously suspect for a receiver to authenticate or disprove it. Either way, there is no shortage of cultural mis/dis on the Internet.

A Plethora of Examples

Rosa Parks ends racism. On December 1, 2013, the Republican National Convention (RNC) tweeted out a photo of Civil Rights icon Rosa Parks, remembering her for her role in the abolishment of racism. Of course, racism is far from over. Belluomini (2014) wonders if the RNC innocently committed a Twitter faux pas with a poorly worded tweet or if the organization is really just ignorant about the state of the world today. Or is this an example of the microaggressions abundantly available online? Sue and colleagues (2007) define microaggressions as "brief and commonplace daily verbal, behavioral, or environmental indignities, whether intentional or unintentional, that communicate hostile, derogatory, or negative racial slights and insults toward people of color" (p. 271). Unfortunately, the literature is rife with information about microaggressions, their negative effects, and people's experiences with them. They certainly happen in person, in all kinds of professional and personal settings, and they are definitely prevalent online. Such is one of the problems in the online sphere of communication and information transfer. This picture made the rounds on Twitter and drew criticism, but that doesn't change the fact that many people saw the original post and maybe thought it true, perhaps because they didn't know who Rosa Parks was or maybe because their worldview suggests that racism doesn't exist.

Native American names deleted off FB. In a similar case of sweeping racial generalizations and a stunning and glaring lack of cultural knowledge, Facebook deleted numerous accounts belonging to Native American users because they supposedly boasted "fake names" (Counter Current News 2014). Ironically, this deletion occurred on Columbus Day, a holiday that celebrates the event that resulted in Native American genocide. With the controversy surrounding sports teams such as the Washington Redskins and the Chicago Blackhawks, which feature die-hard fans fighting to keep these racist names intact, Native Americans with surnames like Creepingbear and Littlefoot shouldn't have such difficulty maintaining their personal accounts on social media.

Racism and Halloween. Despite being treated spuriously on social media, Native American names and costumes are popular every Halloween, when offensive pictures of non-Native people dressed as Indian chiefs and "sexy" Pocahontases pepper social media. Similarly, distasteful pictures of people in blackface are also common. In October 2014, the latest blackface costume depicted professional football player and alleged abuser Ray Rice (Hongo 2014). An assortment of pictures emerged—men in Baltimore Ravens jerseys dragging around blow-up dolls and similarly clad men next to women (also in blackface) with painted on black eyes and bruises, pretending to be Rice's battered wife. Even more disturbing were pictures of young children in the same racist and misogynistic garb. The lessons that racism and misogyny are acceptable, clever, and funny, especially on Halloween, begin early in life.

#IfTheyGunnedMeDown. In the summer of 2014, a young black man was killed by a white police officer in Ferguson, Missouri. Michael Brown's death shared many similarities with the shooting death of Trayvon Martin in 2012 and raised concerns about the status of race relations in the United States. Brown's death, like Martin's, generated a great deal of social media content, some disgraceful and racist and some very meaningful. For example, in the aftermath of Martin's death, a meme circulated featuring people in the Trayvon death pose, referred to as Trayvoning, dressed in hoodies and surrounded by Skittles candies and cans of iced tea. Thereafter, another movement occurred, entitled "We are not Trayvon Martin," in which people posted about their intersectionality (particularly as it is influenced by the larger environment and cultural climate) and privilege, decrying the lack of privilege that contributed to Martin's death (Zimmerman 2013). This is an example of a harmful meme, online message, or image being taken back and used to educate, raise awareness, and protest the status quo.

Similarly, after Brown's death, the #IfTheyGunnedMeDown hashtag appeared on Twitter ("#IfTheyGunnedMeDown" 2014; Stampler 2014). The pictures of Brown peddled by the media show him in a basketball jersey or staring "menacingly" at the camera, and shamefully he was also shown lying dead in the street. The media chose not to show his high school graduation photo, which was taken just weeks before his death. However, the media has often described and shown white suspects in acceptable terms and respectable attire in an effort to paint them as "youth gone wrong" (Wing 2014). #IfTheyGunnedMeDown shows young black adults in their "hood" poses and juxtaposes those images against those showing them in suits, graduation gowns, and military uniforms, and they are smiling, parenting their children, and peacefully living their lives. These photos attempt to dispel some of the stereotypes about black people, black men in particular, and, more importantly, they draw attention to the falsity of images on the Internet. By asking, "What picture do you think the media will use?" these social media users are questioning the accuracy of media coverage and pointing out how damaging mis/dis can be.

The hilarious black neighbors. In the last several years, there have been videos that have gone viral, all of which feature a black person (a neighbor, eyewitness, or even a Good Samaritan) who is interviewed on television and whose mannerisms portray her or him as eccentric, over-the-top, ignorant, and/or buffoon-like. Antoine Dodson's description of a neighborhood robbery (Watson 2010), Sweet Brown's boisterous account of a fire ("Ain't Nobody . . ." 2012), and Charles Ramsey's account of the rescue of three kidnapped women in Ohio (Harris 2013) all made the rounds on YouTube and other social media platforms. They were immediately mocked and turned into minor YouTube celebrities, even having their videos remixed into musical tracks.

Critical Media Consumption through Multiple Literacy Instruction

There is no shortage of mis/dis opportunities on the Internet. And despite the rapid nature of their dissemination and their staying power, many sources and applications can be consulted to verify and refute suspect information. In a more general sense, the bulk of mis/dis on the Internet could be combatted with basic evaluation skills. If consumers of information would take time to make a few simple assessments, mis/dis wouldn't be so prevalent or pervasive. In order to become *critical* consumers of media information, users should:

1. question the currency or date of the information (or lack thereof);
2. consider the plausibility of the information (e.g., can Ebola really turn a person into a zombie if there is no such thing as a zombie?); and
3. consider the reputation of the Web site providing the information[1] (e.g., *The Onion* is a known satire site, so stories with that byline should be treated as fiction even if the headlines and content seem plausible). (Wikipedia provides a list of satirical Web sites: http://en.wikipedia.org /wiki/Category:Satirical_websites.)

Here is another question to consider:

4. Is the information reported elsewhere online?

Although these are seemingly easy questions to ask, critical information consumption is not automatic, and Internet users need to be taught to evaluate, sort, and effectively use the overabundance of information available online. Information consumers also need to be versed in multiple forms of literacy (Daniels 2009, pp. 192–194; Walsh 2010).

Libraries are known for their efforts to promote and enable literacy, particularly when it comes to children and new readers. Perhaps lesser known are their long-standing efforts to facilitate information literacy (Eisenberg et al. 2004; Elmborg 2006), critical information literacy (Bawden and Robinson 2002; Bawden 2008), digital literacy (Lanham 1995; Gilster 1997), and cultural literacy (Ladson-Billings 1995; Overall 2009). Libraries are in the business of sharing information and building knowledgeable communities. Part of this mission is to ensure that constituents are literate in a multitude of areas and are able to seek, differentiate, and select quality information and subsequently to apply that information to their daily lives. Knowledge and understanding of these other literacies will enable online users to be more critical of the information they consume.

Critical Information Literacy

Information literacy is a phrase/concept bandied about in libraries and refers to the ability to read, decipher, evaluate, and use information in everyday life (Kuhlthau 1987). Information literacy is not the same as traditional skills-based literacy; rather, it refers to a frame of reference for consuming information or a type of critical thinking. Information literacy considers the context in which information is found and consumed, and it seeks information that is relevant and that has long-term potential to be useful.

More recent literature and practices in library and information science organizations focus on *critical* information literacy (Elmborg 2006; Tisdell 2008; Accardi, Drabinski, and Kumbier 2010), which extends information literacy by suggesting that in addition to looking at information *in context*, information consumers should consider the underlying power structures that shape the information and the attainment of agency that can come with the acquisition of quality information. Critical information is especially useful when recalling Dinerstein's technocultural matrix (2006, p. 571) and considering why cultural messages in particular are particularly prone to mis/dis.

Digital Literacy/Media Literacy/Visual Literacy

Because this discussion is deliberating mis/dis in the online environment, digital, media, and visual literacy skills are also very important to consider and incorporate. Related concepts, digital, media, and visual literacies are in essence about being "deeply literate in the digital world" and about being "skilled at deciphering complex images and sounds as well as the syntactical subtleties of words" (Lanham 1995, p. 161). Gilster (1997) described *digital literacy* as being about the mastery of ideas, not the mastery of keystrokes. Media literacy narrows in focus somewhat by concentrating on mass media such as television and radio—what is found in popular culture. *Media literacy* can also encompass video games and print products like comic books and graphic novels. *Visual literacy* (also referred to as graphic literacy) is about being able to decipher visual imagery and the intentional and unintentional messages that are projected in them. Visual literacy is not limited to electronically accessed images. This trio of literacies is particularly salient in terms of mis/dis images and messages found online (e.g., memes, videos, etc.).

Cultural Literacy (Cultural Competence)

In some disciplines, cultural literacy is tantamount to being well versed in current events, major points of history, and pop culture. But in the context of this discussion, cultural literacy is interchangeable with cultural competence. Cultural competence is defined as "a highly developed ability to understand and respect cultural differences and to address issues of disparity among diverse populations competently" (Overall 2009, p. 176). This is the definition utilized in the field of library and information science; cultural competence is also discussed in the education, nursing, psychology, counseling, and business management literatures (also known as cultural intelligence) (Cooke 2016).

With this context in mind, cultural literacy can be thought of as information that is reflective of diverse communities and cultural backgrounds. It is a solid grounding in cultural literacy that will be particularly useful when combatting mis/dis as it pertains to cultural messages. For example, thinking back to the racism and Halloween example, it is cultural literacy that will allow an information consumer to really understand how and why the use of blackface is offensive.

CONCLUSION

Everyone is a consumer of information, and everyone should have the basic literacy skills necessary to be critical consumers of information. Becoming multiliterate in a way that is especially effective in the online domain takes practice and diligence, and it begins with learning in the classroom and in libraries. The end goal is to produce critical thinkers and culturally competent users of the Internet. The online world needs more participants who are culture jammers, people who critique popular culture in an effort to challenge the status quo and resist dominant cultural practices (Lasn 1999; Harris 2004; Carducci 2006; Sandlin 2007; Sandlin and Milam 2008). Culture jammers can also counter the mis/dis and perpetuation of racism and stereotypes that often dominate online media.

Tisdell (2008) discusses culture jamming by highlighting films such as *Crash,* Michael Moore's *Sicko*, and Al Gore's documentary, *An Inconvenient Truth*, as important because while they may have evoked uncomfortable feelings or even feelings of anger or denial, they spurred substantive conversations and acknowledgment of important topics affecting society. Just as these movies were catalysts and examples of culture jamming, there are wonderful examples of significant and provocative culture jamming on the Internet. As discussed earlier in the chapter, the #IfTheyGunnedMe-Down campaign was an amazing example of culturally competent and savvy Internet users taking back and redefining part of the narrative that was developing around a tragic event. With this campaign, Twitter users critiqued and challenged the media for promoting negative images of Michael Brown, and then they took their critique a step further by posting multiple and striking images of themselves defying stereotypes. Other examples of culture jamming are evident in sites such as Snopes.com and Know Your Meme; these sites are perhaps not as striking or well-known as the #IfTheyGunned-MeDown campaign, but they provide substantive and detailed information that can be used by consumers seeking to refute mis/dis.

The Internet is also seeing more writers such as Belluomini (2014), who encountered racist mis/dis and challenged herself to learn about microaggressions and their negative repercussions. Her reflection was powerful, and by sharing it with the world, she took a stand against this type of negative information and used her platform to challenge others to do the same. This type of outreach works hand in hand with instructing people in multiple literacies and encouraging them to be critical consumers of information. We need more of these examples, and in order to get them, we need more culturally and digitally literate citizens who are willing, able, and knowledgeable enough to combat cultural mis/dis in the online world.

REFERENCES

Abercrombie, Nicholas, and Brian J. Longhurst. *Audiences: A Sociological Theory of Performance and Imagination.* Thousand Oaks, CA: Sage, 1998.

Accardi, Maria T., Emily Drabinski, and Alana Kumbier (eds.). *Critical Library Instruction: Theories and Methods.* Duluth, MN: Library Juice Press, 2010.

Bawden, David. "Origins and Concepts of Digital Literacy." *Digital Literacies: Concepts, Policies and Practices* 30 (2008): 17–32.

Bawden, David, and Lyn Robinson. "Promoting Literacy in a Digital Age: Approaches to Training for Information Literacy." *Learned Publishing* 15, no. 4 (2002): 297–301.

Brock, Andre. "Life on the Wire: Deconstructing Race on the Internet." *Information, Communication & Society* 12, no. 3 (2009): 344–363.

Carducci, Vince. "Culture Jamming: A Sociological Perspective." *Journal of Consumer Culture* 6, no. 1 (2006): 116–138.

Carey, James. W. "A Cultural Approach to Communication." In James W. Carey (ed.), *Communication as Culture: Essays on Media and Society*, 13–36. New York: Routledge, 1989 [1992].

Cooke, Nicole A. *Information Services to Diverse Populations: Developing Culturally Competent Library Professionals.* Santa Barbara, CA: ABC-CLIO, 2016.

Daniels, Jessie. *Cyber Racism: White Supremacy Online and the New Attack on Civil Rights.* New York: Rowman & Littlefield, 2009.

Dinerstein, Joel. "Technology and Its Discontents: On the Verge of the Posthuman." *American Quarterly* 58, no. 3 (2006): 569–595.

Eisenberg, Michael B., Carrie A. Lowe, and Kathleen L. Spitzer. *Information Literacy: Essential Skills for the Information Age.* Westport, CT: Libraries Unlimited, 2004.

Elmborg, James. "Critical Information Literacy: Implications for Instructional Practice." *The Journal of Academic Librarianship* 32, no. 2 (2006): 192–199.

Fallis, Don. "A Conceptual Analysis of Disinformation." Paper presented at the iConference, 2009. https://www.ideals.illinois.edu/bitstream /handle/2142/15205/fallis_disinfo1.pdf?seq.

Fox, Christopher. *Information and Misinformation. An Investigation of the Notions of Information, Misinformation, Informing, and Misinforming.* Santa Barbara, CA: Praeger, 1983.

Gilster, Paul. *Digital Literacy.* New York: Wiley Computer, 1997.

Harris, Anita (ed.). "Jamming Girl Culture: Young Women and Consumer Citizenship." In *All about the Girl: Culture, Power, and Identity*, 163–172. New York: Routledge, 2004.

Hernon, Peter. "Disinformation and Misinformation through the Internet: Findings of an Exploratory Study." *Government Information Quarterly* 12, no. 2 (1995): 133–139.

Karlova, Natascha A., and Jin Ha Lee. "Notes from the Underground City of Disinformation: A Conceptual Investigation." *Proceedings of the Association for Information Science and Technology* 48, no. 1 (2011): 1–9.

Kuhlthau, Carol C. "Information Skills for an Information Society" (Report ED 297740). Syracuse, NY: ERIC Clearinghouse on Educational Resources, 1987. https://eric.ed.gov/?id=ED297740.

Ladson-Billings, Gloria. "Toward a Theory of Culturally Relevant Pedagogy." *American Educational Research Journal* 32, no. 3 (1995): 465–491.

Lanham, Richard A. "Digital Literacy." *Scientific American* 273, no. 3 (1995): 198–199.

Lankshear, Colin, and Michele Knobel. *New Literacies*. New York: McGraw-Hill Education, 2011.

Lasn, Kalle. *Culture Jam: The Uncooling of America*. New York: Eagle Brook/William Morrow and Co., 1999.

Losee, Robert M. "A Discipline Independent Definition of Information." *Journal of the American Society for Information Science (1986–1998)* 48, no. 3 (1997): 254.

Nakamura, Lisa. "Cultural Difference, Theory and Cyberculture Studies." In *Critical Cyberculture Studies*, 29–36. New York: New York University Press, 2006.

Overall, Patricia Montiel. "Cultural Competence: A Conceptual Framework for Library and Information Science Professionals." *The Library Quarterly* 79, no. 2 (2009): 175–204.

Proctor, Robert, and L. Londa Schiebinger. *Agnotology: The Making and Unmaking of Ignorance*. Stanford, CA: Stanford University Press, 2008.

Rubin, Victoria L. "On Deception and Deception Detection: Content Analysis of Computer-Mediated Stated Beliefs." *Proceedings of the Association for Information Science and Technology* 47, no. 1 (2010): 1–10.

Sandlin, Jennifer A. "Popular Culture, Cultural Resistance, and Anticonsumption Activism: An Exploration of Culture Jamming as Critical Adult Education." *New Directions for Adult and Continuing Education* 2007, no. 115 (2007): 73–82.

Sandlin, Jennifer A., and Jennifer L. Milam. "'Mixing Pop (Culture) and Politics': Cultural Resistance, Culture Jamming, and Anti-Consumption Activism as Critical Public Pedagogy." *Curriculum Inquiry* 38, no. 3 (2008): 323–350.

Sue, Derald Wing, Christina M. Capodilupo, Gina C. Torino, Jennifer M. Bucceri, Aisha Holder, Kevin L. Nadal, and Marta Esquilin. "Racial Microaggressions in Everyday Life: Implications for Clinical Practice." *American Psychologist* 62, no. 4 (2007): 271.

Tisdell, Elizabeth J. "Critical Media Literacy and Transformative Learning: Drawing on Pop Culture and Entertainment Media in Adult Education Practice in Teaching for Diversity." *Transformative Learning: Issues of Difference and Diversity* (2007): 310.

Walczyk, Jeffrey J., Mark A. Runco, Sunny M. Tripp, and Christian E. Smith. "The Creativity of Lying: Divergent Thinking and Ideational

Correlates of the Resolution of Social Dilemmas." *Creativity Research Journal* 20, no. 3 (2008): 328–342.

Walsh, John. "Librarians and Controlling Disinformation: Is Multi-Literacy Instruction the Answer?" *Library Review* 59, no. 7 (2010): 498–511.

Wing, N. (2014). When the Media Treats White Suspects and Killers Better than Black Victims. The Huffington Post Black Voices website: http://www.huffingtonpost.com/2014/08/14/media-black-victims_n_5673291.html.

Zhou, Lina, and Dongsong Zhang. "An Ontology-Supported Misinformation Model: Toward a Digital Misinformation Library." *IEEE Transactions on Systems, Man, and Cybernetics—Part A: Systems and Humans* 37, no. 5 (2007): 804–813.

MEDIA EXAMPLES

"Ain't Nobody Got Time for That." Wikipedia, 23 October 2014. http://en.wikipedia.org/wiki/Ain%27t_Nobody_Got_Time_for_That.

Belluomini, Ellen. "Microaggressions and the Internet." *The New Social Worker*, Spring 2014. http://www.socialworker.com/feature-articles/technology-articles/microaggressions-and-the-internet/.

Counter Current News. "Facebook Deleted Accounts of Native Americans on Columbus Day for Having 'Fake Names,'" 15 October 2014. http://countercurrentnews.com/2014/10/facebook-deleted-accounts-of-native-americans-on-columbus-day/.

Harris, Aisha. "The Troubling Viral Trend of the 'Hilarious' Black Neighbor." Slate, 7 May 2013. http://www.slate.com/blogs/browbeat/2013/05/07/charles_ramsey_amanda_berry_rescuer_becomes_internet_meme_video.html.

Hongo, Hudson. "Ray Rice Halloween Costumes Combine Blackface, Domestic Violence Jokes." Gawker, 26 October 2014. http://gawker.com/ray-rice-halloween-costumes-combine-blackface-domestic-1650963461?utm_campaign=socialflow_gawker_face book&utm_source=gawker_facebook&utm_medium=socialflow.

"#IfTheyGunnedMeDown: Social Media Calls Out MSM for Portrayal of Mike Brown." RT: Question More, 13 August 2014.http://rt.com/usa/179900-if-they-gunned-me-down/.

Stampler, Laura. "Twitter Users Ask What Photo Media Would Use #IfTheyGunnedMeDown." *Time*, 11 August 2014. http://time.com/3100975/iftheygunnedmedown-ferguson-missouri-michael-brown/.

Watson, C. "Antoine Dodson/Bed Intruder." Know Your Meme, 2010. http://knowyourmeme.com/memes/antoine-dodson-bed-intruder.

Zimmerman, Neetzan. "'We Are Not Trayvon Martin' Campaign Turns Protest Meme on Its Head." Gawker, 15 July 2013. http://gawker.com/we-are-not-trayvon-martin-campaign-turns-protest-meme-791571082.

FOUR

From Information Literacy to Full Participation in Society: Through the Lens of Economic Inequality

Mark Winston

Full participation in society—including taking advantage of educational opportunities, making health and other life decisions and career choices, and voting and otherwise engaging in the political process—requires exercising some measure of what some call agency, or the ability to act independently. This requires not only the freedom to make decisions but also the capacity to make informed decisions, with an understanding of the available information.

INTRODUCTION

Information literacy is essential in ensuring that individuals develop the ability to take advantage of opportunities—starting with their being effective consumers of information to supporting sound decision making. The role of librarians relates to addressing the question of information literacy— to what end? Conceptually, the professional principle associated with access to information relates to the goal of ensuring that individuals, ultimately, can be full participants in society. This chapter addresses the leadership role of public libraries in reducing inequities in access to information and in information literacy in order to encourage the goal of full participation in society for individuals, using the example of economic inequality.

Experts and leaders in various arenas have described the enormity and the potential impact of economic inequality, as "a defining issue of our time" (Talley 2014, p. A9). Growing societal discussion of economic inequality has highlighted a U.S. poverty rate that has changed little in 50 years, increasing concentrations of wealth, and declining social mobility throughout the world. And a recent *New York Times* article indicated that, among researchers in the discussion of poverty, "almost forgotten is how many ways poverty plays out in America" (Gabriel 2014). Public policy organizations have emphasized the societal imperative to respond to poverty but also to expand gaps between the rich and poor, for example. The U.S. policy questions related to economic inequality include those involving raising the minimum wage, extending unemployment benefits, a guaranteed minimum income, the income that qualifies workers for overtime, and affordable housing, among others. The research suggests that growing public interest in inequality has influenced policy decisions related to the minimum wage at the state and local levels and wage increases in companies.

In addition, the research has shown the correlation between economic inequality and other measures of social well-being (such as educational attainment and health outcomes) and social participation, such as lower levels of political literacy and political participation among the poor and other marginalized groups. As Amer has noted, for example, "In America the newly developing caste system appears to encompass more than just income inequality, it encompasses inequality in opportunity, in health, in life expectancy, in happiness and in all other aspects of life itself" (Amer 2014). However, despite the expanding research and societal interest in poverty and the decline in social mobility, for example, these issues are rarely described in relation to the importance of information in reducing disparities and encouraging full participation in society. The chapter addresses the leadership role of librarians in fostering literacy in general, information literacy, and other aspects of financial, political, and health literacy, for example, which are often correlated with economic status in order to encourage the goal of full participation in society for individuals.

LITERACY AND FULL PARTICIPATION

Basic literacy is seen as foundational—as "'a fundamental human right and the foundation for lifelong learning,' according to UNESCO. 'It is fully essential to social and human development in its ability to transform lives'" (Rölz 2016). Conceptually, the idea of literacy—developing facility and comfort with understanding the written word—is particularly important

as a part of full participation. The Organization for Economic Coopera-
tion and Development's (OECD) Program for the International Assessment
of Adult Competencies (PIAAC) "broadly defines literacy as 'understanding, evaluating, using, and engaging with written text to participate in society,
to achieve one's goals, and to develop one's knowledge and potential'" (Kena
et al. 2014). The relationship between literacy and information literacy
appears to be indicated implicitly in this definition. In addition, the OECD
identifies literacy, as well as "problem solving" as "information processing
skills" (Kena et al. 2014). Similarly, it has been noted, "Economic security,
access to health care, and the ability to actively participate in civic life all
depend on an individual's ability to read" (Huffpost 2013). And UNESCO
has indicated that "a literate community is a dynamic community, one that
exchanges ideas and engages in debate" (Rölz 2016).

In this regard, full participation in society—including taking advantage
of educational opportunities, making health and other life decisions and
career choices, and voting and otherwise engaging in the political process—
requires exercising some measure of what some call agency, or the ability
to act independently. This requires not only the freedom to make decisions
but also the capacity to make informed decisions, with an understanding
of the available information. In a context that includes the exponential
expansion in the amount of information and the range of information sources
around which individuals must navigate and from which they must select,
the extent to which literacy is the norm is important to consider.

In an article entitled "The U.S. Illiteracy Rate Hasn't Changed in
10 Years," research by the U.S. Department of Education and the National
Institute for Literacy indicated that "32 million adults in the U.S. can't read.
That's 14 percent of the population. 21 percent of adults in the U.S. read
below a 5th grade level, and 19 percent of high school graduates can't read"
(HuffPost 2013). Also, in recent results, "Eighteen percent of U.S. adults
performed at the lowest level of the PIAAC literacy scale." And civics or
political science content has been deemphasized in K–12 curricula overtime (Kena et al. 2014).

In the library and information science literature, the discussion of economic inequality has focused primarily on library services to the poor and
the intersection of economic inequality and the digital divide, with limited
consideration of issues related to collections and pertinent resources to support research, with the exception of reviews of the many books published
on economic inequality and discussions of subject headings related to
poverty.

In this regard, public libraries are in a position to foster access to information and to otherwise address disparities in information literacy and related areas, given the pervasiveness of economic inequality. Inasmuch as the public library, which has been referred to as the "people's university," operates as both an educational and a cultural institution, the mission allows the opportunity to address issues of literacy independently and in collaboration with other organizations, through collections, library services, and programming. For example, public libraries are well positioned to collaborate with literacy councils, which may focus on some combination of services related to adult literacy, English for Speakers of Other Languages (ESOL) programs, and preparation for citizenship tests. While libraries are often viewed positively as a result of their neutrality with regard to the development of collections across a range of topics, including those considered controversial and fostering the free exchange of ideas, libraries are also more likely to be viewed as neutral for adult learners, who are more likely to be uncomfortable with entering a Literacy Council building or an alternative/nontraditional school setting for assistance than they would be in entering a library for literacy-related education. It is certainly the case that in addition to formalized partnerships, literacy tutors often choose library locations for individual and group tutoring sessions with students.

Public libraries are also in the position to provide information literacy (and related) instruction in a range of formats—from one-on-one assistance with patrons to basic and advanced technology classes, including those related to catalog, database, and Web searching, as well as the development of instructional guides and resources made available online via library Web sites.

And for adult learners, libraries can promote access to information and actively develop programming on career options, standardized testing, college admissions, and financial aid, as well as information sessions on individual colleges and universities, trade schools, and other training programs, such as Job Corps and AmeriCorps.

In areas related to health literacy, the range of programming that public libraries can provide, as well as the information that they make available, can substantively support learning and decision making among individuals. Potential partners include nonprofit health services, hospitals, and other health providers and experts, from physicians and public health specialists to nutritionists and wellness coaches.

Here, collaboration with nonprofits and educational institutions can be critical in providing programming and services in areas related to other aspects of full participation. For example, collaboration with nonprofits that focus on college preparation, such as college access centers (on locating information on potential majors and the outlook for professions, for example) can be of particular value, including for high school and college students, in supplementing the roles of guidance counselors and career placement offices. However, the reach of nonprofit organizations that offer assistance with job search, resume development, and understanding of basic technology skills, such as those related to completing and submitting online job applications and sending attachments, can be supported by the library, not just in relation to programming but also in providing access to computers and Internet access.

And the library is also in a position to provide venues for instruction for both testing services and test preparation services, particularly when these services are offered without cost, in order to reach the broadest audience.

However, economic inequality can prevent people from being able to take full advantage of opportunities for personal success and happiness. What exactly is economic inequality? The following sections will outline what it is and how it affects large sections of the U.S. population.

ECONOMIC INEQUALITY

Conceptually, economic inequality includes a focus on income inequality and disparities in wealth. Worldwide, political, religious, and economic policy leaders have said that economic inequality is potentially "a defining issue of our time" (Talley 2014). In the United States, a recent *Washington Post* article referred to the "experts who see inequality as one of the most urgent moral, political and economic long term challenges facing the country" (Sargent 2013).

The study of economic inequality reflects the breadth, depth, and the interdisciplinarity of the research and research questions in this area. The research ranges from the gathering and study of basic demographic data to the analysis of trend data related to poverty, hunger, unemployment, wealth, income, and social mobility, for example. Also, studies address differences and disparities among segments of the population related to race or ethnicity and to poverty, mobility, and wealth, for example. The research also considers questions related to the causes of poverty and declining levels of social mobility and includes studies of public opinion related to aspects of economic inequality, for example. Public opinion research, for instance, has revealed that, among members of the general public, "Concerns about inequality are at a 25-year high" (Hargreaves 2014). And there is the strong indication of the relationship between growing public interest in and concern about economic inequality and the success of ballot measures related to the minimum wage at the state and local levels and wage increases in quite a number of companies (Linn 2013; Hiscott 2014; Vinik 2014).

Here, broad and expanding interest in increased understanding of issues of economic inequality, among researchers across disciplines, policy makers, and members of the general public, is reflected in the extensive dissemination of findings, analyses, and discussion in scholarly and general interest publications and in media coverage. For example, a number of highly publicized research reports, including *The Shriver Report* on the economic status of women (Shriver and Center for American Progress 2014), a *Time* magazine cover story analyzing studies of social mobility (Foroohar 2011), and a recent study on the concentration of wealth by the international organization Oxfam (Cohen 2015), have expanded societal discussion of issues of economic inequality in general and in relation to specific segments of the population.

Generally speaking, in the United States and more broadly, the research indicates a U.S. poverty rate that has changed little in 50 years and increasing concentrations of wealth and declining levels of social mobility throughout the world. Even with economic progress and more safety net programs, in 2013, in the United States, "the official poverty rate was 14.5 percent . . . [with] 45.3 million people in poverty" (U.S. Census Bureau 2014), as compared with the "nearly 13 percent of the population . . . living below the poverty level" (Lohr 2008) in 1968.

In addition, the introduction and expanded use of terms, such as "food insecurity" and "food deserts," reflect the current context in relation to poverty. The U.S. Department of Agriculture reports nearly 50 million people in "food-insecure households" (2015). Using the official definition, "these households were uncertain of having, or unable to acquire, enough food to meet the needs of all their members because they had insufficient money or other resources for food" (Department of Agriculture 2015).

In relation to income inequality, particularly in the United States, the average CEO earns 347 times more than the average worker and over 700 times more than individuals earning minimum wage (AFL-CIO 2017). Overall, the top 1 percent of earners receive more than 20 percent "of all pretax income, while the bottom 90%'s share is below 50%" (DeSilver 2013). And according to the Center on Budget and Policy Priorities,

"Wealth—the value of a household's property and financial assets, minus the value of its debts—is much more highly concentrated than income. The best survey data show that the top 3 percent of the distribution hold over half of all wealth" (Stone, Trisi, Sherman, and DeBot 2014).

Looking worldwide, according to the 2015 Oxfam research report:

> The 80 wealthiest people in the world altogether own $1.9 trillion, the report found, nearly the same amount shared by the 3.5 billion people who occupy the bottom half of the world's income scale. . . . The type of inequality that currently characterizes the world's economies is unlike anything seen in recent years. (Cohen 2015)

The extent of wealth inequality in the United States has been represented in relation to that of other countries in the world, such that "now, the wealth gap in the United States is the forth [sic] highest in the world; only Russia, the Ukraine and Lebanon are worse" (Amer 2014).

The demographics research also addresses questions, such as how segments of the population differ. For example, research considers the percentage of the poor population that is white, the percentage of women and children who live near or below the poverty line, how politicians and other policy makers differ from the average American, and the wealth of whites, as compared with blacks and Latinos.

According to *The Shriver Report*, "a third of all American women are living at or near a space we call 'the brink of poverty.' We define this as less than 200 percent of the federal poverty line, or about $47,000 per year for a family of four" (2014). Census data further indicate that 20 percent of children in the United States live in poverty (U.S. Census Bureau 2014).

The research also addresses racial disparities in terms of economic inequality. While most of those in the United States who are poor are white, in terms of income, "more than one in four blacks live in poverty, while fewer than one in 10 whites do" (Luhby 2014a). African Americans also have lower incomes, a rate of unemployment that is twice as high (Luhby 2014a), and less wealth as well. "A typical black household has accumulated less than one-tenth of the wealth of a typical white one" (Luhby 2014).

Similar disparities in income and unemployment have been documented for Hispanics, in comparison with whites. And, in the case of wealth, "Hispanics make up 16.3% of the U.S. population, but own only 2.2% of its wealth" (Luhby 2014b). The disparities are also reflected in the nature of the wealth. In this regard, "during the economic downturn, Hispanics suffered larger losses than other groups because housing made up a greater share of their assets" (Luhby 2014b).

WHAT THE RESEARCH TELLS US ABOUT THE EFFECTS OF ECONOMIC INEQUALITY

It is important for librarians working to mitigate the effects of economic inequality to know that the economic inequality research is frequently characterized by its complexity and ambiguity. One illustration of the conflicting research findings relates to the question of whether upward mobility in the United States is declining substantially over time, as the *Time* magazine cover story, based on the analysis of studies of social mobility, indicates (Foroohar 2011) or remaining relatively constant (Chetty and Hendren 2015). There is substantial agreement, however, regarding the fact that economic or social mobility "is consistently lower" (Chetty and Hendren 2015) and "significantly lower in the United States than in most" similar countries (Zakaria 2011).

Among those who address the decline in social mobility in the United States, Amer indicates that in the developing "caste system," "your origins, and particularly your family's fortunes can in large part determine your future. If you were born rich you are likely to remain that way. But, if you were born poor, you and your progeny are likely to remain that way as well" (2014).

While researchers wrestle with the question of causality (whether variable A causes variable B or whether the two are simply related, while other factors contribute to causing B), the research does indicate the relationship between measures of economic inequality and other measures of social well-being.

In research related to educational performance and attainment and criminal penalties, for example:

> In 2013, approximately 10.9 million school-age children 5 to 17 years old were in families living in poverty. Research suggests that living in poverty during early childhood is associated with lower than average academic performance that begins in kindergarten and extends through elementary and high school. Living in poverty during early childhood is associated with lower than average rates of school completion. (Kena et al. 2014)

In addition, the data indicate that a small percentage of the poor population in the United States—only about 4 percent of individuals from low-income backgrounds—graduate from college (Alexander, Entwisle, and Olson 2014). In "Another Edge for the Wealthy," the author discusses the results of a recent study that indicated the extent to which "demonstrated interest" weighs heavily in admissions decisions among colleges and universities (Jaschik 2017). And among factors such as campus visits, speaking with a university staff person at a college fair, or calling the university with questions, the study "found that colleges most favor demonstrated interest of the kind that costs money" (Jaschik 2017). Similarly, attorney Brian Stevenson of the Equal Justice Initiative has described "a criminal justice system that treats you better if you're rich and guilty than if you're poor and innocent" ("Bryan Stevenson" 2000). The poor are more likely to be targeted, arrested, charged, receive subpar representation, and receive harsher penalties for the same offense than are their middle-class and wealthier counterparts (Quigley 2015).

With regard to health outcomes and health literacy, those "most likely to experience low health literacy are older adults, racial and ethnic minorities, people with less than a high school degree or GED certificate, people with low income levels, non-native speakers of English, and people with compromised health status" (National Center for Education Statistics 2006). In August 2017, results of a recent study revealed that "The Mediterranean Diet Works—But Not If You're Poor." Despite the positive health effects associated with the types of recommendations associated with the Mediterranean diet, such as substantial consumption of fruits, vegetables, and whole grains, "it matters what kind of foods you pick within its framework, how that food was grown and how you prepare it" (Judkis 2017). Results indicate the correlation between income and the ability to access and purchase a "variety" of foods and more nutrient-rich and safer organic options. The research "also found a link between education and healthy eating, suggesting that programs to teach low-socioeconomic status people how to choose and prepare cheap meals—and the benefits they can derive from such choices—are important" (Judkis 2017).

In terms of participation, while the research reflects "disappointing" levels of political literacy in the United States, generally, the research indicates far lower levels of political literacy (Romano 2011) and participation of the poor in influencing the political and policy making processes, including those affecting them directly. In expressing appreciation of economic inequality and the difference in their own economic circumstances, some members of Congress and other politicians took part in the SNAP (Food

Stamp) Challenge and, subsequently, in the Minimum Wage Challenge in order to illustrate the effort required to survive on an extremely small food budget or minimal income and to increase their understanding of the experience of the poor.

Writer Malcolm Gladwell summarizes a key aspect of the complexity of the economic inequality research, in terms of causality in research related to mobility. He notes, "What effect does where you live have on how you turn out? It's a difficult question to answer because the characteristics of place and the characteristics of the people who happen to live in that place are hard to untangle" (Gladwell 2015)

Amer (2014) has noted that:

> The children of the rich grow up in better environments. They live, for the most part, in two-parent homes, get better nutrition, and receive better health care and better elementary education. They grow up healthier both physically and psychologically and are, in many ways, better suited for life in today's society. In addition, the rich can afford to send their children to the better universities, which are now beyond the reach of most high school graduates.

Researchers, such as Zakaria, describe countries in Europe, for example, that "have made serious investments to create equality of opportunity for all. They typically have extremely good childhood health and nutrition programs, and they have far better public education systems than the United States does. As a result, poor children compete on a more equal footing against the rich" (2011). He contends that, by comparison, "In the United States, however, if you are born into poverty, you are highly likely to have malnutrition, childhood sicknesses and a bad education" (2011). As a result, inequality leads to effects that are often perpetuating.

Researchers have indicated the broad connection between literacy and economic inequality, noting, for example, "Literacy is a crucial socio-economic factor in poverty" (Rölz 2016). And John Miller, longtime literacy researcher, has said that "literate behaviors are critical to the success of individuals and nations in the knowledge-based economies that define our global future" (Strauss 2016).

CONCLUSION

Of the pervasive challenges that have been indicated by the research and in statements made by leaders in various arenas, economic inequality is clearly one of the major issues facing the United States and the world, and it has clear ties to literacy. With nearly 15 percent of Americans, including at least 20 percent of children in the United States, living in poverty, with even higher percentages among African Americans and Hispanics, less social mobility in the United States than is the case in similar countries, and widening gaps in wealth and income between the rich and poor throughout the world, the growing societal problem of economic inequality has been well documented. In addition, the correlation between poverty and other measures of well-being has been shown in the research in a range of areas.

However, the fact that the societal and research-based discussion of economic inequality rarely addresses the extent to which access to information is a primary consideration in the lives of individuals. This omission represents an opportunity for libraries to play a key role in addressing this connection, which is, in fact, frequently suggested strongly in the ways in which literacy is defined as, essentially, information literacy.

To a large extent, this chapter emphasizes the relationship between economic inequality and other aspects of social well-being because of the particular relevance of that relationship to the role of libraries. As economic inequality (and poverty in particular) are correlated to individuals' health and health literacy and political participation and political literacy, for example, there is value in integrating the thinking about these issues in the design of public library programs, services, and collections. In this regard, focusing on the individual aspects of literacy, information literacy, and health literacy, for example, under the broader or more overarching goal of fostering full participation, given libraries' role related to information, provides a framework for implementing practical initiatives that reflect the mission of libraries and the importance of assuring that one of society's most pervasive issues is considered holistically by an organization that is positioned to reduce disparities and enhance full participation in society.

REFERENCES

AFL-CIO. "Executive PayWatch: High-Paid CEOs and the Low-Wage Economy." Executive PayWatch, 2017. https://aflcio.org/paywatch.

Alexander, Karl L., Doris Entwisle, and Linda Olson. *The Long Shadow: Family Background, Disadvantaged Urban Youth, and the Transition to Adulthood*. New York: American Sociological Association, 2014.

Amer, Sam. "The Developing New American Caste System." OpEDNews, 7 January 2014. http://www.opednews.com/articles/The-Developing -New-America-by-Sam-Amer-American-Crossroads_American -Exceptionalism_American-Foreign-Policy_American-World-Service -Corps-140107-718.html.

"Bryan Stevenson: Equal Justice Initiative." *Religion & Ethics Newsweekly*, 30 June 2000. http://www.pbs.org/wnet/religionandethics/2000/06 /30/june-30-2000-bryan-stevenson-equal-justice-initiative/11076.

Chetty, Raj, and Nathaniel Hendren. "The Impacts of Neighborhoods on Intergenerational Mobility: Childhood Exposure Effects and County-Level Estimates." Equality of Opportunity Project, Harvard University and NBER, 2015. www.equality-of-opportunity.org/assets /documents/nbhds_slides.pptx.

Cohen, Patricia. "Oxfam Study Finds Richest 1% Is Likely to Control Half of Global Wealth by 2016." *Business Day*, 19 January 2015. http:// www.nytimes.com/2015/01/19/business/richest-1-percent-likely-to -control-half-of-global-wealth-by-2016-study-finds.html?_r=0.

DeSilver, Drew. "U.S. Income Inequality, on Rise for Decades, Is Now Highest Since 1928." Pew Research Center, 5 December 2013. http:// www.pewresearch.org/fact-tank/2013/12/05/u-s-income-inequality -on-rise-for-decades-is-now-highest-since-1928.

Foroohar, Rana. "What Ever Happened to Upward Mobility? Why the U.S. Has Become the Land of Less Opportunity—and What We Can Do to Revive the American Dream." *Time*, 14 November 2011. http:// content.time.com/time/magazine/article/0,9171,2098584,00.html.

Gabriel, Trip. "50 Years into the War on Poverty, Hardship Hits Back." *New York Times*, 20 April 2014. https://www.nytimes.com/2014/04/21/us /50-years-into-the-war-on-poverty-hardship-hits-back.html.

Gladwell, Malcolm. "Starting Over: Many Katrina Victims Left New Orleans for Good. What Can We Learn from Them?" *New Yorker*, 24 August 2015. http://www.newyorker.com/magazine/2015/08/24 /starting-over-dept-of-social-studies-malcolm-gladwell.

Hargreaves, Steve. "America's Love/Hate Relationship with the Rich," CNN Money, 18 June 2014. http://money.cnn.com/2014/06/18/luxury/rich -love-hate/index.html.

Hiscott, Rebecca. "7 Companies That Aren't Waiting for Congress to Raise the Minimum Wage." HuffPost, 26 June 2014. http://www.huffing tonpost.com/2014/06/26/companies-minimum-wage_n_5530835 .html.

HuffPost. "The U.S. Illiteracy Rate Hasn't Changed in 10 Years," 6 September 2013. https://www.huffingtonpost.com/2013/09/06/illiteracy-rate_n_3880355.html.

Jaschik, Scott. "Another Edge for the Wealthy." Inside Higher Ed, 27 July 2017. https://www.insidehighered.com/news/2017/07/27/study-says-common-admissions-practice-measuring-demonstrated-interest-favors.

Judkis, Maura. "The Mediterranean Diet Works—But Not If You're Poor, A Study Finds." *Washington Post*, 3 August 2017. https://www.washingtonpost.com/news/food/wp/2017/08/03/the-mediterranean-diet-works-but-not-if-youre-poor-a-study-finds/?utm_term=.be87a75b1147.

Kena, Grace, Susan Aud, Frank Johnson, Xiaolei Wang, Jijun Zhang, Amy Rathbun, Sidney Flicker-Wilkinson, Paul Kristapovich, Liz Notter, and Virginia Rosario. "The Condition of Education 2014." U.S. Department of Education, National Center for Education Statistics, 28 May 2014. https://nces.ed.gov/pubsearch/pubsinfo.asp?pubid=2014083.

Linn, Allison. "Minimum Wage Worker Protests Raise Awareness—But What about Paychecks?" NBC News, 13 December 2013. http://www.nbcnews.com/feature/in-plain-sight/minimum-wage-worker-protests-raise-awareness-what-about-paychecks-v21878491.

Lohr, Kathy. "Poor People's Campaign: A Dream Unfulfilled," NPR, 19 June 2008. http://www.npr.org/templates/story/story.php?storyId=91626373.

Luhby, Tami. "5 Disturbing Stats on Black-White Inequality," CNN Money, 21 August 2014a. http://money.cnn.com/2014/08/21/news/economy/black-white-inequality/index.html?iid=HP_LN.

Luhby, Tami. "Hispanics' Massive Wealth Gap," CNN Money, 10 July 2014b. http://money.cnn.com/2014/07/10/news/economy/hispanics-wealth/index.html.

National Center for Education Statistics. 2006. *The Health Literacy of America's Adults: Results from the 2003 National Assessment of Adult Literacy*. Washington, DC: U.S. Department of Education, 2006. https://nces.ed.gov/pubs2006/2006483.pdf.

Quigley, Bill. 2015. "40 Reasons Why Our Jails Are Full of Black and Poor People." HuffPost, 2 June 2015. http://www.huffingtonpost.com/bill-quigley/40-reasons-why-our-jails-are-full-of-black-and-poor-people_b_7492902.html.

Rölz, Isabella. "How Literacy Reduces Poverty." The Borgen Project, February 2016.https://borgenproject.org/how-literacy-reduces-poverty.

Romano, A. 2011. "How Dumb Are We?" *Newsweek* 157, no. 13/14: 56–60.

Sargent, Greg. "Inequality Is 'The Defining Issue of Our Time.'" *Washington Post*, The Plum Line, 4 December 2013. https://www.washingtonpost.com/blogs/plum-line/wp/2013/12/04/inequality-is-the-defining-issue-of-our-time/?utm_term=.31492dbfccc6.

Shriver, Maria, and Center for American Progress. "The Shriver Report: A Woman's Nation Pushes Back from the Brink: Executive Summary," *Washington Post*, 12 January 2014. http://shriverreport.org/a-womans-nation-pushes-back-from-the-brink-executive-summary-maria-shriver.

Stone, Chad, Danilo Trisi, Arloc Sherman, and Brandon DeBot. 2014. "A Guide to Statistics on Historical Trends in Income Inequality." Center on Budget and Policy Priorities, 10 December 2014. http://www.cbpp.org/cms/?fa=view&id=3629.

Strauss, Valerie. "Most Literate Nation in the World? Not the U.S., New Ranking Says." *Washington Post*, 8 March 2016. https://www.washingtonpost.com/news/answer-sheet/wp/2016/03/08/most-literate-nation-in-the-world-not-the-u-s-new-ranking-says/?utm_term=.1daf9f627ade.

Talley, Ian. "IMF Warns Inequality Is a Drag on Growth: Says Rising Income Inequality Is Weighing on Global Economic Growth." *Wall Street Journal*, 13 March 2014.

United States Census Bureau. "Income and Poverty in the United States: 2013," 16 September 2014. https://www.census.gov/library/publications/2014/demo/p60-249.html.

United States Department of Agriculture Economic Research Service. "Key Statistics & Graphics: Food Security Status of U.S. Households in 2013," 12 January 2015. http://www.ers.usda.gov/topics/food-nutrition-assistance/food-security-in-the-us/key-statistics-graphics.aspx.

Vinik, Danny. "Minimum Wage: The One Piece of Bad News for Republicans Last Night." The New Republic, 5 November 2014. http://www.newrepublic.com/article/120135/midterm-elections-show-minimum-wage-hike-good-politics.

Zakaria, Fareed. "The Downward Path of Upward Mobility." *Washington Post*, 9 November 2011. http://www.washingtonpost.com/opinions/the-downward-path-of-upward-mobility/2011/11/09/gIQAegpS6M_story.html.

FIVE

Misinformation and Intellectual Freedom in Libraries

Shannon M. Oltmann

Misinformation will always be present—and it will sometimes be in our libraries.

Intellectual freedom is a core value of librarianship and is fundamental to the work of librarians (ALA 2004b). Free and open access to a wide variety of materials allows individuals to seek whatever information they desire, creating autonomy and well-rounded citizens. As professionals, we argue that intellectual freedom is an essential component of an informed citizenry, which is important for a healthy democracy. Does this acceptance of a wide range of views extend to fake news and misinformation? This chapter will argue that, like other types of information, fake news should not be censored. The best way to combat fake news is not by silencing it but by creating information-literate individuals who can effectively and independently evaluate news sources.

INTELLECTUAL FREEDOM BASICS

Intellectual freedom is "the right of every individual to both seek and receive information from all points of view without restriction. It provides for free access to all expressions of ideas through which any and all sides of a question, cause or movement may be explored" (American Library Association [ALA] 2017b, para. 1). To put it another way, "The American

Library Association promotes the freedom to choose or the freedom to express one's opinions even if that opinion might be considered unorthodox or unpopular, and stresses the importance of ensuring the availability of those viewpoints to all who wish to read them" (ALA 2017a, para. 1).

This right to receive information and explore ideas is derived from the First Amendment to the U.S. Constitution. The First Amendment protects individuals' right to freedom of speech, and that includes the right to access information (see Oltmann 2016a for a fuller explanation). As Smolla (2005) notes, "While we usually think of the First Amendment as empowering speakers to speak, it might well be understood as embracing a concomitant right of listeners to listen, viewers to view, or readers to read" (pp. 2–72). This right to access information exists "even when unconnected to any specific willing speaker or any specific instance of speech" (Blitz 2006, p. 818). Libraries of all types are important locations for exercising this freedom.

The complexities of information access can be seen in a 1992 court case *Kreimer v. Bureau of Police for Morristown*. In this case, Richard Kreimer, a homeless patron, was repeatedly ejected from the public library in Morristown, New Jersey, for offensive body odor and nuisance behavior, in accordance with library rules. He challenged these rules, arguing that they restricted his ability to use a public space and access information. The courts ruled that the library had the right to set some behavioral guidelines but also recognized that "libraries are the quintessential locus of the receipt of information" (p. 1256). Libraries could not make rules for the purpose of excluding certain patrons, even problematic ones; all people deserved access to information in a library.

In another case, the Island Trees Union Free School District of Long Island, New York, voted to remove seven books from the school library because they were perceived as anti-American and filthy (*Pico v. Board of Education* 1982). The books included *Slaughterhouse-Five* (by Kurt Vonnegut Jr.), *The Naked Ape* (Desmond Morris), *Down These Mean Streets* (Piri Thomas), *Best Short Stories of Negro Writers* (edited by Langston Hughes), *Go Ask Alice* (anonymous), *Laughing Boy* (Oliver LaFarge), *Black Boy* (Richard Wright), *A Hero Ain't Nothin' but a Sandwich* (Alice Childress), *Soul on Ice* (Eldridge Cleaver), *A Reader for Writers* (edited by Jerome Archer), and *The Fixer* (Bernard Malamud).

The Supreme Court ruled that libraries (especially school libraries) have discretion about which books they decide to put into the collection, but once an item is in the collection, it cannot be removed merely because people disagree with its content. In other words, the school board in this case was wrong to remove the books, and the books were reinstated into the library. The justices stated that the right to access information was "an inherent corollary of the rights of free speech."

Intellectual freedom has been a central focus of the library profession (Gorman 2000) and of the American Library Association (ALA) since 1939, when the Library Bill of Rights was first adopted. The Library Bill of Rights is our profession's explanation of intellectual freedom and how it guides our services. (See http://www.ala.org/advocacy/intfreedom/librarybill.)

In addition to the Library Bill of Rights, the ALA has adopted over 25 "interpretations" of this document; these interpretations provide detailed guidance on how to apply the Library Bill of Rights in specific circumstances. Different interpretations explain intellectual freedom in relation to academic libraries, library access for minors, exhibit spaces, rating systems, and more. For example, in "Access for Children and Young Adults to Nonprint Materials," the ALA (ALA 2004a, para. 7) states that minors have a right to access library content in all formats. The statement goes on to say, "The interests of young people, like those of adults, are not limited by subject, theme, or level of sophistication. Librarians have a responsibility to ensure young people's access to materials and services that reflect diversity of content and format sufficient to meet their needs."

To summarize the meaning of intellectual freedom, no material should be excluded from libraries simply because of its perspective or stance (or the stance of its creator), especially when it comes to partisan or doctrinal issues. All points of view should be represented in the library, even if they are unpleasant or unpopular. Thus, some libraries contain books written by current or former terrorists, white supremacists, and anarchists. Some libraries include materials that deny the occurrence of the Holocaust during World War II. Some libraries offer materials that advocate for trying to convert lesbian and gay individuals to heterosexuality—and some libraries have resources that rebut this so-called conversion therapy.

Not all of these perspectives belong in *every* library; that is a collection development decision that needs to be made by each individual library. The point here is that all of these views have a home in *some* library. It does not mean that these views—or any view present in a library—are endorsed and supported by the library.

Another part of intellectual freedom is neutrality. This is demonstrated in two ways: by having all points of view present and by not endorsing a particular set of views. Such a stance may be especially valuable in times of sociopolitical contention.

INTELLECTUAL FREEDOM AND CENSORSHIP

Another important part of intellectual freedom is resistance to censorship. The ALA defines censorship as "the suppression of ideas and information that certain persons—individuals, groups or government officials—find objectionable or dangerous" (ALA 2017b, para. 3). Censorship can be seen as the inverse of intellectual freedom: Intellectual freedom advocates for all points of view to be present, while censorship wants to prevent certain views from being present. Censorship can happen in many ways. Two of the most common ways for libraries are challenges and self-censorship.

A materials challenge (or request for reconsideration) means that a patron (or a group of patrons) objects to certain material in the library and lodges a formal objection. Often, there is a form to be filled out. Some libraries review the material, often with a committee, then determine whether the material in question should be kept, relocated, or withdrawn. Other libraries, fearful of conflict or upsetting patrons, simply remove items that have been challenged. The ALA strongly opposes this latter approach; more information, as well as resources to combat challenges, can be found at the Challenge Support page of the ALA Web site (http://www.ala.org/tools /challengesupport). According to the ALA:

> A challenge is an attempt to remove or restrict materials, based upon the objections of a person or group. A banning is the removal of those materials. Challenges do not simply involve a person expressing a point of view; rather, they are an attempt to remove material from the curriculum or library, thereby restricting the access of others. (ALA 2017a, para. 2)

The Office of Intellectual Freedom (OIF) of the ALA collects reports of challenges every year; in 2016, 323 challenges were reported to OIF, but they estimate that most challenges go unreported.

Self-censorship in a library context occurs when librarians censor certain viewpoints. Some librarians may decide to not purchase items that are (or may be) controversial even though they otherwise fit the library's collection development policy. For example, some librarians resist purchasing books with main characters who are lesbian, gay, bisexual, or transgender even though these books may be popular, well written, and appropriate for the library's patrons. Other times, librarians place materials in a location other than where they should be, such as putting a teen book in the adult section. This may be done because of the content, but it effectively makes the material more difficult to locate and functions as censorship. It is not clear how often self-censorship occurs. One study found that 70 percent of school librarians admitted to some self-censorship (Whelan 2009). However, another study of public librarians in the Midwestern United States found that 11.4 percent of respondents reported that they avoided purchasing something because they thought it might be challenged (Oltmann forthcoming). Even though we don't know the exact rate of occurrence, we do know that some self-censorship happens in all types of libraries.

Because of the importance of intellectual freedom, librarians ought to resist both materials challenges and self-censorship. Intellectual freedom is one of the foundations of modern librarianship, and it stands in opposition to censorship of all kinds.

INTELLECTUAL FREEDOM AND DEMOCRACY

One reason that intellectual freedom is so important has to do with democracy. As the ALA says, "Intellectual freedom is the basis for our democratic system. We expect our people to be self-governors. But to do so responsibly, our citizenry must be well-informed. Libraries provide the ideas and information, in a variety of formats, to allow people to inform themselves" (ALA 2017b, para. 2).

In a democracy, the people are considered the "governors," meaning that the power of the government rests in the hands of the people. Politicians are voted into and out of office; this is the main power that people have, though they can exercise power in other ways as well (such as writing letters, contacting their representatives, or protesting). The strength of a democracy thus relies on people acting as good governors, being responsible with the power they have.

Intellectual freedom ensures that a wide variety of information is available, representing many different points of view. When many perspectives are available, people can become educated on a wide range of issues and viewpoints. For example, many libraries will have resources that address conflict-torn parts of the world; some books may advocate for military intervention, others for nonmilitary humanitarian action, and yet others for no intervention at all. Some resources may call for international coalitions (such as acting through the United Nations), while others may suggest acting alone.

People can access this range of perspectives, gain new information, and evaluate the various arguments on multiple sides of important issues. As a result of their reading and reflection, people may decide to write their representatives, petition for specific actions, protest other actions, or change their voting plans. In these ways, they can exercise their power and guide the direction of the democracy.

Of course, we can acknowledge that people in a democracy don't always exercise their power responsibly. Some people don't vote; some people vote but not in an informed manner. People may not take advantage of the varied information available in their local library. Nonetheless, supplying a wide variety of viewpoints is still significant: we should strive to enable the ideal actions (that is, people exercising their power in an informed way), even if it doesn't always happen.

WHAT ABOUT FAKE NEWS?

The previous discussion makes the need for an assured right to information access clear. It is essential for several reasons, including the need to help enhance the democratic process. From this perspective, it may seem logical to think that libraries should have only the most accurate, relevant, and meaningful information, designed to specifically be of assistance to voters who want to learn and be engaged. However, limiting a library collection in this manner would be inherently dangerous and shortsighted. Simply put, fake news and misinformation cannot simply be excluded from a library.

That does not mean any and all sources of fake news and misinformation must be in every library. But it does mean the decision to exclude something cannot be taken lightly or easily.

First, recall the Library Bill of Rights (ALA 2017c). Librarians have an ethical duty to avoid excluding resources simply due to their viewpoint or the viewpoint of the author. In the words of Asheim (1953), "To the selector, the important thing is to find reasons to keep the book. Given such a guiding principle, the selector looks for values, for strengths, for virtues which will overshadow minor objections." Librarians are trained to include good resources for their libraries. In contrast, says Asheim, *censors* look for reasons to exclude books.

In addition, the definition of fake news is contested and unsettled. (Even within this book, the term is used in different ways!) It's also politically fraught, with adopters of different political perspectives using the term in different ways. Because of this, librarians can't rely on the terminology. Just because something has been called fake news does not mean it can be excluded.

Instead, it must be evaluated on its own merits. This is where the library's collection development policy can be extremely useful. (If you are working in a library that lacks a collection development policy, you should work on developing one as soon as possible.) Most collection development policies include accuracy or truthfulness as a factor to consider when evaluating a potential purchase. Sometimes quality is another factor for consideration. Thus, items can be evaluated on these grounds. Many items that spread misinformation will not pass muster when assessed according to collection development guidelines.

Nonetheless, some items that are controversial and that may be considered fake news or misinformation may still become part of a library's collection. There are numerous reasons for this. It may be seen as necessary to have a well-rounded collection. To represent all views, some questionable material may have to be accepted. When this happens, that librarians may make several responses, but perhaps the most effective and meaningful response is to improve your patrons' information literacy.

Information literacy, including critical literacy, is discussed elsewhere in this book, so this chapter will not explain it at great length. However, it is worth noting that patrons who are information literate and confident in those skills are less likely to fall prey to misinformation. Instead, they will be able to evaluate and recognize it for what it is. In turn, information-literate individuals often help others with gaining access to information, creating a potential ripple effect of information literacy and overall reducing the effects of fake news. This is one of the most important reasons to teach information literacy to one's patrons. Misinformation will always be present—and it will sometimes be in our libraries. Information literacy is the best tool to combat its presence.

PUTTING THESE PRINCIPLES INTO PRACTICE

For some librarians, the ideals of intellectual freedom sound challenging to enact. That is, some people appreciate the concepts of intellectual freedom and resisting censorship but struggle with how to put these ideas into practice. Defending intellectual freedom, especially in relation to misleading or biased information, can often be difficult, but the following incidents will provide further illumination as to how this can be done.

One intriguing case took place in Miami, Florida, in 2006. Parents challenged the inclusion of a children's book, *Vamos a Cuba*, in the school libraries because it did not accurately depict the oppression and difficulty of life in communist Cuba (Aguayo 2006). The book, one in a series, portrayed a holiday in Cuba, but many Cuban ex-patriates living in Miami-Dade County saw the book as inaccurate and misleading. Despite recommendations from two committees to keep the book, the school board decided to remove *Vamos a Cuba* and the other 23 books in the series.

The ACLU filed suit, arguing that this was contradictory to the decision rendered in *Pico vs. Board of Education* (1982). The 11th Circuit Court ruled that the book removal was acceptable, though many legal scholars and library experts disagree with the ruling (Fiore 2011). The school board argued the books were removed due to inaccuracies, but many believed the books were removed due to disagreement with their message—that is, the book did not condemn communism in Cuba. Under the guidelines established in the *Pico* case, removal due to inaccuracy would be acceptable, while removal because of partisan disapproval would not be.

Similarly complicated, confusing issues arose more recently with the children's books *A Fine Dessert: Four Centuries, Four Families, One Delicious Treat* (by Emily Jenkins and Sophie Blackall) and *A Birthday Cake for George Washington* (by Ramin Ganeshram). Both of these books were criticized for the simplistic portrayal of slavery. For example, in *A Fine Dessert*, slaves are shown smiling while baking the dessert for the master's family, then hiding in the cupboard to lick the bowl clean. The main characters in *A Birthday Cake*, likewise, are slaves, depicted as resourceful, proud, and happy—though an author's note explains that the main character escaped slavery, leaving his daughter behind. *A Fine Dessert* was published first and received positive reviews initially before being scrutinized more carefully. The first author, Jenkins, eventually came to regret her book and its insensitive portrayal of slavery (Smith 2016). When *A Birthday Cake* was released, it faced criticism almost immediately, and the publisher soon pulled the book (Peralta 2016).

Libraries faced uncertainty with these books—should they be purchased? If they were purchased and then subjected to criticism and suspended publication, should they be withdrawn? If left on the shelves, should a caution or explanatory note be offered? Libraries have answered these questions differently, depending on their community, their collection development policy, and the stance of their director or board. Few libraries own either book, as a simple search on WorldCat reveals. Often the books, if purchased, were withdrawn from the library collection due to perceived inaccuracies. Librarians generally hesitate to put "warnings" on books, as this can be seen as a form of label (which the ALA opposes) or as a way to prejudice the reader against a book. While the ALA did not issue formal guidance regarding these books, the National Coalition Against Censorship (NCAC) did oppose withdrawing the books.

On the other hand, some books are withdrawn amid support for this move. One such book is *Arming America: The Origins of a National Gun Culture* (2000) by Michael A. Bellesiles. Although the book received positive reviews initially, including winning the Bancroft Prize, its claims were soon called into question. Other historians noted fabrications, falsehoods, and problems with citations (see McLemee 2010 for a summary). The controversy led the prize committee to rescind the Bancroft Prize and Bellesiles to resign from Emory University. Although many academic and public libraries had initially purchased *Arming America*, today few (if any) still retain copies. This was a book that was proven to have fabrications and outright lies. It thus did not meet collection development policies that included accuracy as one consideration for inclusion.

One final example is worth considering. In their research into book challenges in public libraries and schools, Oltmann, Peterson, and Knox (2017) uncovered a challenge to a nonfiction book in an Alabaman public library. One patron complained that a book, *The Seventies: The Great Shift in American Culture, Society, and Politics* (by Bruce Shulman), falsely depicted the rock band Lynyrd Skynyrd as racist. After reviewing the title, the director recommended retaining the book but adding additional resources to provide another perspective. This is often the most appropriate way to deal with content that may be perceived to have some bias. Supplementing the collection with additional viewpoints provides more information so that patrons can develop their own, informed views.

CONCLUSION

Librarianship has taken a strong stance in favor of intellectual freedom and opposing censorship. Libraries try to include a wide range of views on a wide range of subjects. This has implications for democracy: Including diverse perspectives creates the opportunity for the public to be more well-rounded and better educated, leading to more informed actions at the polls. The difficulty arises when we consider misinformation or fake news; intellectual freedom dictates that we cannot automatically reject such sources. Instead, they must be carefully considered in light of the mission of the library and its collection development policy. Indeed, misinformation will always be present—and will sometimes be in our libraries. Creating information-literate patrons is the best tool to combat its presence.

REFERENCES

Aguayo, Terry. "Miami-Dade School Board Bans Cuba Book." *New York Times*, 16 June 2006. http://www.nytimes.com/2006/06/16/edu cation/16cuba.html.

American Library Association (ALA). "Access for Children and Young Adults to Nonprint Materials," 2004a.http://www.ala.org/advocacy /intfreedom/librarybill/interpretations/accesschildren.

American Library Association (ALA). "Core Values of Librarianship," 2004b. http://www.ala.org/advocacy/intfreedom/corevalues.

American Library Association (ALA). "Banned and Challenged Books," 2017a. http://www.ala.org/advocacy/bbooks/about.

American Library Association (ALA). "Intellectual Freedom and Censor-ship Q&A," 2017b. http://www.ala.org/advocacy/intfreedom/censor ship/faq.

American Library Association (ALA). "Library Bill of Rights," 2017c. http://www.ala.org/advocacy/intfreedom/librarybill.

Asheim, Lester. "Not Censorship but Selection." *Wilson Library Bulletin* 28, no. 1 (1953): 63–67.

Blitz, Marc Jonathan. "Constitutional Safeguards for Silent Experiments in Living: Libraries, the Right to Read, and a First Amendment The-ory for an Unaccompanied Right to Receive Information." *UMKC L. Rev.* 74 (2006): 799.

Fiore, Katherine. "ACLU v. Miami-Dade County School Board: Reading Pico Imprecisely, Writing Undue Restrictions on Public School Library Books, and Adding to the Collection of Students' First Amendment Right Violations." *Vill. L. Rev.* 56 (2011): 97.

Gorman, Michael. *Our Enduring Values.* Chicago: American Library Asso-ciation, 2000.

Kreimer v. Bureau of Police for Morristown. 1992. 958 F.2d 1242.

McLemee, Scott. "Amazing Disgrace." *Inside Higher Ed*, 19 May 2010. https://www.insidehighered.com/views/2010/05/19/amazing -disgrace.

Oltmann, Shannon M. "Intellectual Freedom and Freedom of Speech: Three Theoretical Perspectives." *The Library Quarterly* 86, no. 2 (2016a): 153–171.

Oltmann, Shannon M., Chris Peterson, and Emily J. M. Knox. "Analyzing Challenges to Library Materials: An Incomplete Picture." *Public Library Quarterly* 36, no. 4 (2017): 274–292.

Oltmann, Shannon M. (forthcoming). "Important Factors in Midwestern Public Librarians' Views on Intellectual Freedom." *Library Quarterly.*

Peralta, E. Amid Controversy, Scholastic Pulls Picture Book about Washington's Slave. *NPR*, 18 January 2016. https://www.npr.org/sections /thetwo-way/2016/01/18/463488364/amid-controversy-scholastic -pulls-picture-book-about-washingtons-slave.

Pico v. Board of Education. 1982. 457 U.S. 853.

Smith, V. Smiling Slaves in a Post–*A Fine Dessert* World: Figuring out Intelligent People Can Disagree. *Kirkus Reviews*, 4 January 2016. https://www.kirkusreviews.com/features/smiling-slaves-post-fine -dessert-world.

Smolla, Rodney A. *Smolla and Nimmer on Freedom of Speech*, Volumes I and II. Danvers: Thomson/West, 2005.

Whelan, D. L. 2009. "A Dirty Little Secret: Self-Censorship." *School Library Journal* 55, no. 2: 26–30.

SIX

Fighting Fake News: The Limits of Critical Thinking and Free Speech

Kay Mathiesen

> While critical thinking is indeed an important weapon in our arsenal to fight the problem of fake news, critical thinking is not without drawbacks and is likely to be limited in its effectiveness in combating fake news.

*   *   *

> If critical thinking were all that were needed for people to get quality information, there would be little need for the librarian.

During the U.S. 2016 presidential election, the following headline, "Pope Francis Shocks World, Endorses Trump for President," received 960,000 "engagements" (e.g., clicks, likes, shares, and comments) on Facebook. Indeed, such fake news stories about the election received more engagements on Facebook than the top election stories from major news outlets, such as *The New York Times* and *CNN* (Silverman 2016b). Some argue that such stories swayed the 2016 American election (Parkinson 2016), though research has thrown some doubt on that claim (Allcott and Gentzkow 2017). For library and information professionals in a "political system that depends on an informed citizenry" (Kranich 2001), fake news poses a serious problem. And belonging to a profession that "significantly influences or controls the selection, organization, preservation, and dissemination of information" (American Library Association [ALA] 2008), librarians have an important role to play in trying to address this problem. This chapter considers how we as a society and as library and information professionals in particular should respond to the problem of fake news. In particular, it asks whether, as many have suggested, increased critical thinking is the best or only answer. And it considers whether more direct interventions to lessen the amount of fake news are violations of the rights of freedom of speech.

The chapter begins with a proposed definition of fake news, noting the harm that fake news may do to people as individuals and citizens. It then considers the common suggestion that we should respond to fake news with an increased emphasis on the importance of critical thinking. It is argued that, while critical thinking is indeed an important weapon in our arsenal to fight the problem of fake news, critical thinking is not without drawbacks and is likely to be limited in its effectiveness in combating fake news. To determine whether more direct interventions to block or otherwise lessen the effect of fake news should be rejected as a violation of freedom of speech, John Stuart Mill's argument for freedom of thought and expression is presented. Through a careful application of Mill's reasoning to the case of fake news, it is shown argued that fake news ought not be afforded the same protections from various forms of intervention (such as changing, blocking, or labeling) that cover other forms of speech.

WHAT IS FAKE NEWS?

The term "fake news" came into our national consciousness during the 2016 election. But what is fake news? Some use it as a term of abuse for any reporting they disagree with. This has led some pundits to argue that we should stop using the term altogether (Hupke 2017). Whatever you call it, however, fake news points to an important phenomenon that needs exploration. It is, as the name suggests, "fake" news—false or misleading[1] information that is made to look like "real news." Here we can think of real news as "material reported in a newspaper or news periodical or on a newscast" (*Merriam-Webster* 2018), as well as online versions thereof, that is the product of journalistic practice, that is, "the activity of gathering, assessing, creating, and presenting [current] information," where "'getting it right' is the foundation upon which everything else is built" (American Press Institute 2018). Of course, all real news sources will fall short of the ideal of what news journalism should be: They can be biased, make mistakes, and there may even be individual reporters who make up sources or stories. But real news outlets try to meet at least some of the standards of journalism as put forward in journalism schools and professional organizations such as the American Press Institute, and they are expected to make corrections and apologize when they fall short.

Fake news is perhaps best understood as *counterfeit* news, originating from a *fraudulent* news source. Fake news, thus, is not really "news" any more than a counterfeit currency is money. Fake news gets traction by fooling people into thinking it has the social and epistemic[2] legitimacy of real news. In other words, it is made to look like or sound like legitimate news. For example, if someone puts a flyer on your car saying that Martians have invaded, that is not fake news. It is false information or misinformation, yes. It may even be disinformation if the person intends to deceive. But virtually no one would mistake the flyer for a news report.

The other defining characteristic of fake news, as the term is used here, is that the motivation of its authors is to get some sort of gain or advantage not necessarily related to persuading the audience that the "news" is true (Associated Press 2016; Sydell, 2016). To illustrate this point, consider the two most significant forms of fake news. First, there is the fake news produced by those who find it profitable. For instance, the original author of the "Pope Endorses Trump" story had an Adsense ID[3] connected to a wide range of sites. These sites garnered traffic (and thus profit) with made-up "news" items that had both high name recognition and a strong local interest (e.g., "Eminem Explains Why He Is Moving to Salina, Kansas"). These sites pretended to be the online presence of local television news stations, with names such as "Dailynews5.com," "WTOE5News.com," "WRPT News Network," and "Daily News 11" (Silverman and Singer-Vine 2016). The purpose of making up these stories, as well as the pope endorsement story, was to drive Web traffic to the sites and thereby to make money from the Adsense account (Ohlheiser 2016). It was irrelevant whether anyone ended up believing the stories; all that mattered is that people clicked on them.

Second, fake news is produced as part of a general disinformation campaign. For instance, the goal of many Russian so-called troll farms was not to convince Americans to adopt policies friendly to the Russian government, as would be the case with traditional propaganda. Instead, its goal was to sow confusion and create greater divisions within American society (Scott 2017).

THE HARM FAKE NEWS DOES

Fake news has the potential to undermine core values of autonomy, democracy, trust, and the common good. Autonomy (literally meaning "self-rule") is the ability to make decisions for ourselves based on our own goals and values and to carry these out free from unwarranted interference.

Fake news may undermine individuals' autonomy by misleading them, thereby making it harder for them to act according to their goals and values. As a number of philosophers have pointed out, if we are acting on inaccurate information, then our choices are unlikely to truly express our interests and values. As Hill puts it, "[O]pportunities for rational, self-controlled living are restricted when one does not know the realities of one's choice situations" (Hill 1991, p. 36).

The most obvious examples of this are fake news stories related to health. One of the top health news stories about HPV (human papillomavirus vaccine), with the most shares, likes, and comments, falsely reported that the College of Pediatricians issued a warning about the HPV vaccine (Forster 2017). Parents, who want to do what is best for the health of their children, may rely on such information and choose not to vaccinate them—putting their children at greater risk of developing various cancers.

Fake news also has the potential to undermine individual autonomy by making people less likely to trust legitimate news sources. In order to determine their goals and pursue them effectively, people need accurate information. If those we trust do not provide us with this information, we will remain ignorant or in doubt. There is evidence that the proliferation of fake news is indeed making people less likely to trust the news they hear. A recent study in the UK (Cooke 2017) showed that this particularly hurt the trust people put in news found on social media. This is troubling given that 67 percent of Americans get at least some of their news from social media (Shearer and Gotfried 2017). While some degree of skepticism is autonomy enhancing, wide-scale distrust is not. Distrust leaves us unable to rely on obtaining the information we need to make important decisions about our lives.

Not only does fake news undermine the autonomy of individuals, it undermines the common good by creating situations where some act on incorrect information and create harm to themselves and others. An infamous example was the so-called Pizzagate case, where someone took a gun and went to a Washington, D.C., pizza place, convinced that it was a cover for a Hilary Clinton–linked pedophile ring (Silverman 2016a). Fake news also undermines the common good by deceiving people in power, who in turn may believe it and make decisions on the basis of incorrect information. For example, it would not be surprising if Donald Trump's executive decisions, not just his tweets, were influenced by the fake news he consumes (Goldmacher 2017).

In addition to undermining autonomy and the common good, fake news undermines democracy by depriving people of the accurate information that they need to make political decisions that best reflect their individual and collective interests. As James Madison (1910 [1822], p. 903) famously put it, "A popular government without popular information or the means of acquiring it, is but a prologue to a farce, or a tragedy, or perhaps both. And a people who mean to be their own Governors, must arm themselves with the power which knowledge gives." In other words, if the people are going to be in charge, they need to have knowledge about what is going on. Fake news makes it more difficult to determine what the truth is. For instance, a recent Pew Research Center study found that 64 percent of Americans think fake news is sowing confusion about facts related to current events (Barthel, Mitchell, and Holcomb 2016).

CRITICAL THINKING AND ITS BENEFITS

The most commonly suggested solution for the problem of fake news is more critical thinking (e.g., Baldoni 2018). The thought is that, if people were better critical thinkers, then they wouldn't be fooled by fake news. Librarians often speak about information literacy in this context, rather than critical thinking. However, critical thinking is a key component to information literacy and is most relevant in the case of fighting fake news. We need critical thinking when searching for, understanding, and evaluating information—in particular, "documentary" information of various sorts.

The term "critical thinking" is widely used, but it can be a difficult concept to pin down. There are a number of different definitions of critical thinking, some of which are quite complex. For example, according to a recent Delphi expert study, critical thinking is "purposeful, self-regulatory judgment which results in interpretation, analysis, evaluation, and inference, as well as explanation of the evidential, conceptual, methodological, criteriological, or contextual considerations upon which that judgment is based" (Facione and Gittens 2015, p. 27). It would require some serious critical thinking just to understand what that means!

It may be more helpful to start with the simpler definition suggested by Beyer (1985): *"Critical thinking is defined as the process of determining the authenticity, accuracy, and worth of information or knowledge claims."* Depending on the particular case, engaging in critical thinking as defined by Beyer may require skills of interpretation, analysis, evaluation, inference, and the like that were listed in the Delphi Study.

Improving people's critical thinking is lauded not just for its epistemic consequences—helping us to properly assess sources and claims and thereby to avoid error—it is also praised for various ethical advantages. First, critical thinking is praised as nonpartisan. It is a process or method of approaching various knowledge claims objectively, not from the point of view of a set of rigid beliefs. Second, critical thinking is thought to protect people's autonomy by allowing them to make their own decisions about what information to access, share, and believe. Third, critical thinking is seen as a way that individuals can help both themselves and society at large. If people are trained in critical thinking, they will be less likely to spread false information to others, thus lessening the potential harm to society posed by false information.

BEING CRITICAL ABOUT CRITICAL THINKING

In order to determine to what extent critical thinking may be a solution to the problem of fake news, it is important that we think critically about claims for the value of critical thinking. Are these claims accurate? Are they the whole truth about critical thinking, or only part of the truth? As we will see, the case for critical thinking is pretty strong, but it glosses over many complications. Any intervention, including training people in critical thinking, has limitations and unintended consequences. And any intervention may be good in principle but may have serious drawbacks or limitations when used by fallible human beings.

First, even though the teachers of critical thinking—be it a librarian or a Web site—do not try to sway people about what to believe; they do hope to sway *how* people evaluate sources. Guidelines, in order to be at all helpful, are not going to be neutral about what counts as a "good source." Consider, for example, the International Federation of Library Associations and Institutions' infographic, "How to Spot Fake News" (based on a Factcheck .org article by Kiely and Robertson (2017). Among others, it provides the following suggestions for how to think critically and avoid fake news:

1. *Check the date.* Reposting old news stories doesn't mean they're relevant to current events.

2. *Check the author.* Do a quick search on the author. Are they credible? Are they real?

3. *Check your biases.* Consider whether your own beliefs could affect your judgment.

Notice that this advice is based on a number of assumptions that may not be true in particular cases and that, if applied consistently, might lead to problematic bias. The advice in suggestion 1, for example, assumes that the best information about something is the most recent. But as a general rule, this is obviously false. It may be true of news reports on issues where things are rapidly changing and new facts are frequently coming to light—although, even in such cases, old reporting may contain important background information. However, the focus on currency is much less likely to be true of other sorts of information—such as analysis or research. In those cases, it is the quality of the work itself, not necessarily its newness that makes the difference. Of course, assessments of quality are much more difficult to make than determining how long since something was first published.

The advice in suggestion 2 assumes that the best information comes from established authors or sources with a track record that can attest to their credibility. This may hold true in many cases. But, if followed blindly, it could lead to ignoring fresh perspectives from new voices. In addition, it would eliminate works by anonymous writers altogether. There are many cases where anonymity is necessary in order for people to speak the truth. Indeed, James Madison, Alexander Hamilton, and John Jay wrote the Federalist Papers anonymously, partly for fear that, if they were known to be the authors, their arguments would be rejected based on that fact alone (Ekstrand and Jeyaram 2011).

The advice in suggestion 3 says that you should consider whether your own beliefs are affecting your judgment. This is good advice for checking your biases. There are a couple of problems/limitations to this advice, however. First, it is good to be aware of your biases, but your *beliefs* should affect our judgment. Indeed, that is key to critical thinking: We must use what we already know about the world to determine whether something we are reading is credible. Second, there are serious limitations in our ability to see our own biases. As numerous studies in social science show, even the best critical thinkers among us find it very difficult to be aware of their own blind spots and biases (West, Meserve, and Stanovich 2012).

Of course, all of these suggestions can be useful if people are careful to apply them appropriately and recognize their limitations (or our limited ability to put them into practice). It is important that we keep in mind, however, that critical thinking is not simple and that no method of critical thinking is completely neutral. This is a criticism not of critical thinking per se but of overly optimistic claims for it as a panacea.

Moreover, viewing individual critical thinking as the sole answer to our shared epistemic threats, such as fake news, may actually serve to *undermine* autonomy. While traditionally autonomy has been thought of as something purely individual, in fact, genuine autonomy requires a particular kind of social environment. Feminist work on "relational autonomy" has shown how genuine autonomy requires specific social conditions (Mackenzie and Stoljar 2000). In particular, autonomy requires a cooperative environment, where we can trust others. For example, if we are forced to do everything on our own, then we will have very little time to engage in the variety of activities or go deeply into any one activity—a serious restriction on our ability to live our lives according to our own lights.

Here is how relational autonomy plays out in the context of seeking and evaluating information: As human beings, we have a limited amount of time in our lives to accomplish our goals and fulfill our obligations. The time we spend on any one good, such as thoroughly researching a topic, is necessarily time we do not spend on something else. It is unreasonable to expect each individual to spend a significant amount of time fact-checking everything they hear or read (Christiano 1996). Indeed, the economist Anthony Downs (1957) famously argued that people do not spend much time seeking further information on political topics, nor, given the influence of their vote, is it clear that they should. If people do not spend much time seeking relevant information, then it is very unlikely that they will spend a lot of time *evaluating* information. This is why society needs information intermediaries, such as journalists and librarians. As Ranganathan's 4th Law of Library Science reminds us, the job of the information professional is to "Save the time of the reader" (1931, p. 337). If critical thinking were all that is needed for people to get quality information, there would be little need for the librarian.

To conclude, critical thinking, though essential, is not a solution without drawbacks and limitations. Given this, perhaps we should consider whether other ways of dealing with fake news should also be implemented. However, most of the recommendations for other solutions—such as labeling, annotating, delinking, and blocking fake news stories and sites—look a lot like acts of censorship that librarians rightly abhor. In the rest of this chapter, I will argue that fake news is a special case where freedom of speech is not harmed by such apparently censorious measures.

JOHN STUART MILL'S DEFENSE OF FREEDOM OF EXPRESSION

Undoubtedly the most influential defense of freedom of expression and access to information is John Stuart Mill's chapter "On Liberty of Thought and Discussion" from his seminal *On Liberty* (1978 [1859]). In that work, he argued that we should not restrict speech simply because we think is false. Since the main objection to fake news is its falsity, we will focus on his arguments to see if they apply (or fail to apply) to the case of fake news.

Mill's argument proceeds by considering a case where we want to censor some information because it is false. He explains how such censorship can do more harm than good. First of all, Mill points out that the information you believe to be false *could* be true. Humans are fallible; we frequently make mistakes in our assessment of whether something is true. We know that people have erred in the past when they censored things that turned out to be true.[4] For instance, the Catholic Church attempted to stop Galileo from asserting that the earth goes around the sun because they believed that his assertion was false, as it contradicted scriptural authority (Johnston 2008).

Second, Mill argues that, even if we are right that the information we wish to censor is in the main false, there could also be some truths in it. And if we censor it, we may lose those pieces of the truth for a long time, to our own detriment. For example, in an effort to prove false theories (e.g., the circularity of the orbits of the planets, the fixity of the species, the superiority of the white race, the nonexistence of the Holocaust), people have been motivated to engage in research to support their theories. In the course of this research, they may have gathered many accurate observations. While all these *theories* are false and by themselves add nothing to useful knowledge, it would be a mistake to censor these works, according to Mill, because in so doing, we would also be censoring the many accurate observations that could contribute to our knowledge of the truth.

Third, even in cases where we are correct and the information is completely false, Mill believed that it will do more harm than good if we censor it. We need to know what these falsehoods are in order to expose them. If we forbid people from expressing false and repulsive views, we will drive the proponents of these views underground, depriving them and everyone else of the opportunity to hear opposing arguments and evidence. Furthermore, we will harm ourselves by losing an opportunity to restate and defend our core beliefs and values. Mill argued that it is only by regularly bringing before our minds the reasons that support our beliefs that we can truly know and live by our beliefs. If we are not challenged by others to debate and defend our beliefs, they become what Mill calls "dead dogmas"—things we believe but with no true understanding of their meaning or importance.

To sum up Mill's argument: If we want a society that is grounded on as much truth as we are at this time capable of achieving, then we should not censor views that we think false. First, we are not infallible—the view we wish to suppress may be true. Second, even if the view is unquestionably false, it may contain some elements of the truth. Third, even in cases where we are actually correct that the information is completely false, it will do more harm than good to censor it. It will deprive us of the opportunity to bring more clearly before our minds our reasons for rejecting it, and it will deprive those who believe it from hearing any opposing evidence and arguments.

WHY MILL'S ARGUMENT DOES NOT APPLY TO FAKE NEWS

Mill is pretty convincing that we ought to avoid censoring communications that we believe to be false. However, it can be shown that Mill's arguments do not apply to the case of fake news. In order to show this, we need to answer three questions: Is fake news harmful? Is there a reasonable chance that fake news can be true or at least partially true? Is there social value in arguing against the claims made in fake news reports?

So, let's begin with the first question: Is fake news harmful? As discussed earlier in the chapter, there are strong reasons to think that fake news can and sometimes does cause harm. Of course, the fact that fake news may cause harm is not, by itself, a sufficient reason to attempt to restrict it. Any speech can cause harm to others by (perhaps inadvertently), leading them to believe something that they would be better off not believing. This is the case even for true speech. For example, correctly knowing how to go about doing something (e.g., eating fire, breaking blocks with a karate chop) is not the same as being advisable to try it. So, while the fact that fake news is harmful gives us some reason to intervene, it does not give us a decisive reason to do so if there are compelling reasons *not* to do so. Whether this is the case depends on the answers to the next two questions.

Is there a reasonable chance that fake news is true or at least has some new truths in it? The answer to this is clearly no. At worst, the information contained in fake news is intentionally created to deceive and thus is designed to be false. At best, it is created with no concern for whether it is true or false—in which case it would be mere chance if it happened to be true. It may contain some banal facts easily obtained elsewhere, such as that Francis was pope and Donald Trump was running for president of the United States, but it is not to be expected that it contains any new truths. To expect the information presented in fake news to be true is like expecting one of the monkeys in the proverbial room full monkeys at typewriters to produce "Hamlet": It could happen, but the odds are so low that it would be foolish to base any of our decisions on that expectation.

So we come to our final question: Is there social value in arguing against the claims made in fake news reports? There seems good reason to think that it would actually be a complete waste of time. To begin with, in the cases we are considering, fake news does not reflect the beliefs of anyone. Engaging in debate over the claims made in fake news will not have the value of potentially changing anyone's mind. Furthermore, fake news does not provide the opportunity for enlightening discussion that results from a back-and-forth sharing of ideas that Mill had in mind.[5] Furthermore, engaging in discussion and debate about fake news is likely to redirect our attention from important real debates on matters of substance. Indeed, wasting our time may be the point of some forms of fake news. As the *Handbook of Russian Information Warfare* (Giles 2016) points out, *getting people to waste lots of time sorting through disinformation is one of the goals of those who produce it.*

Of course, there are other arguments for why we ought not to censor—namely, because it violates the individual right to freedom of thought and expression (Scanlon, 1972; Dworkin 1978, pp. 232–244), because information is necessary in a democracy (Meiklejohn 1948), or simply because we don't want governments deciding which information we access and don't access. However, none of these arguments works in the case of fake news either. First, no one's right to freedom of thought and expression is at stake in the case of fake news because the people who are spreading the information *do not believe what they are saying.* In interfering with their speech, we are only preventing them from doing something they wish to do—for example, to make money from advertisers or to get people to waste time and make bad decisions.

Second, while debating different opinions on policy and accessing factual information are necessary for a democracy to thrive, fake news provides neither of these. And, third, most of the suggestions for how to combat fake news are not directed to government agencies but to corporate entities such as Facebook, Google, and Twitter. Furthermore, even if the government were to create regulations to reduce the amount of fake news, this would be justified in order to prevent an intentional and harmful fraud upon the public. Recall that fake news is "counterfeit" news. It is a con and a fraud. The U.S. Supreme Court has held that fraud is not covered by the First Amendment (Liebmann, 2014).

CONCLUSION AND RECOMMENDATIONS

Given the limitations of critical thinking as a solution to fake news and the fact that fake news ought not enjoy the same sorts of speech protections as other forms of speech, we should consider other interventions that could supplement the critical thinking approach. A number of interventions are possible at the level of governmental law and policy or of corporate decision making and technological/social design. Indeed, many different approaches are already being tried, from fact-checking to blocking known fake news Web sites (Guynn 2017).

There are, moreover, a number of steps that librarians and other information professionals can also take to combat fake news. Educating users about critical thinking is an important first step, but here are some others that might be considered:

- Individually and collectively work to create norms on social media platforms around thoughtful sharing and "liking" information. Consider the epistemic impact of your sharing practices and encourage others to do so.

- Stay informed about efforts to curb the influence of fake news. Note research-backed approaches. Take advantage of these approaches when possible. For example, one recent study showed that people who are likely to consume and believe fake news rarely go to fact-checking Web sites (Guess, Nyhan, and Reifler 2018). Thus, relying on such systems alone to fight fake news is unlikely to be effective.

- Support the creation of tools that enable individuals to easily spot or block fake news. For instance, a system called NewsGuard, which would provide expert ratings of the overall accuracy of news Web sites, is currently in the works. Unlike fact-checking sites like Scopes and Politifact, it would provide the rating right next to the search results. It may be available as an add-on that libraries could include on their computers.

- Create and support the use of aids for determining the accuracy and source of information. Look for ways to make it easier for users to find high-quality information sources and avoid low-quality sources. In addition to NewsGuard, a number of automated systems to identify potential fake news are currently in the testing stages (Snow 2017; Graves 2018).

- Inform the public about the problem of fake news, while avoiding politically polarizing cases and language.

- Support reasonable measures by governments and corporate actors to reduce the amount of fake news displayed by search engines and social media sites. A recent report by the Brookings Institution suggested that, in addition to making it easier for consumers to spot fake news, media technology companies should "make it hard to monetize" fake news by removing the financial incentive of online advertising from fake news sites (West 2017). These are responses that the government could encourage with Federal Trade Commission regulations.

NOTES

1. Of course, it is possible for fake news to be true and not misleading, but this would in most cases will be purely accidental or part of a technique to better disguises itself as legitimate news.

2. "Epistemic" refers to those processes or states that are related to knowledge. So, for example, something has a high epistemic value if it effectively promotes the acquisition of knowledge.

3. Adsense is a service provided by Google that allows owners of Web sites to place advertisements on their Web pages and earn money based on the number of visits to the pages or clicks on the advertisements.

4. Note that Mill's argument does not rely on any skepticism about whether there are truths. Mill assumed that, although they can be difficult to determine and we can make a lot of mistakes, we can discover truths and that knowledge can improve our lives.

5. Of course, once fake news is spread, then we may need to spend time debunking its claims, but this is only because it was allowed to spread in the first place. No one would believe it, if it were not posted and spread.

REFERENCES

Allcott, Hunt, and Matthew Gentzkow. "Social Media and Fake News in the 2016 Election." *The Journal of Economic Perspectives* 21, no. 2 (2017): 11–21.

American Library Association (ALA). "Code of Ethics," 2008. http://www.ala.org/tools/ethics.

American Press Institute. "The Elements of Journalism," 2018.https://www.americanpressinstitute.org/journalism-essentials/what-is-journalism/elements-journalism/.

Associated Press. "In Macedonia's Fake News Hub, This Teen Shows How
    It's Done." CBS News, 2 December 2016. http://www.cbsnews.com
    /news/fake-news-macedonia-teen-shows-how-its-done.
Baldoni, John. "How to Use Your Brain to Defeat Fake News." *Forbes*, 7
    February 2018. https://www.forbes.com/sites/johnbaldoni/2018/02
    /07/how-to-use-your-brain-to-defeat-fake-news.
Barthel, Michael, Amy Mitchell, and Jesse Holcomb. "Many Americans
    Believe Fake News Is Sowing Confusion." Pew Research Center,
    15 December 2016. http://www.journalism.org/2016/12/15/many
    -americans-believe-fake-news-is-sowing-confusion.
Beyer, Barry K. "Critical Thinking: What Is It?" *Social Education* 49, no. 4
    (April 1985): 270–276.
Christiano, Thomas. 1996. *The Rule of the Many: Fundamental Issues in
    Democratic Theory*. Boulder, CO: Westview Press.
Cooke, Kristy. "'Fake News' Reinforces Trust in Mainstream News Brands."
    Kantar.com, 31 October 2017. https://uk.kantar.com/business/brands
    /2017/trust-in-news/.
Downs, Anthony. "An Economic Theory of Political Action in a Democ-
    racy." *Journal of Political Economy* 65, no. 2 (1957): 135–150.
Dworkin, Ronald. 1978. *Taking Rights Seriously*. Cambridge, MA: Harvard
    University Press.
Economist. "Fake News: You Ain't Seen Nothing Yet." *Economist*, 1 July
    2017. https://www.economist.com/news/science-and-technology
    /21724370-generating-convincing-audio-and-video-fake-events
    -fake-news-you-aint-seen.
Ekstrand, Victoria Smith, and Cassandra Imfeld Jeyaram. "Our Founding
    Anonymity: Anonymous Speech during the Constitutional Debate."
    American Journalism 28, no. 3 (2011): 35–60.
Facione, Peter, and Carol Ann Gittens. 2015. *Think critically*. New York:
    Pearson.
Forster, Katie. "Revealed: How Dangerous Fake Health News Conquered
    Facebook." *Independent*, 7 January 2017. http://www.independent
    .co.uk/life-style/health-and-families/health-news/fake-news-health
    -facebook-cruel-damaging-social-media-mike-adams-natural-health
    -ranger-conspiracy-a7498201.html.
Giles, Keir. *Handbook of Russian Information Warfare*. Rome: NATO
    Defense College, 2016.
Goldmacher, Shane. "How Trump Gets His Fake News." *Politico*, 15
    May 2017. https://www.politico.com/story/2017/05/15/donald-trump
    -fake-news-238379.

Graves, Lucas. "Factsheet: Understanding the Promise and Limits of Automated Fact-Checking." Reuters Institute for the Study of Journalism, 2018. http://www.digitalnewsreport.org/publications/2018/factsheet-understanding-promise-limits-automated-fact-checking/.

Guess, Andrew, Brendan Nyhan, and Jason Reifler. "Selective Exposure to Misinformation: Evidence from the Consumption of Fake News during the 2016 US Presidential Campaign." European Research Council, 9 January 2018. https://www.dartmouth.edu/~nyhan/fake-news-2016.pdf.

Guynn, Jessica. "Facebook Begins Flagging 'Disputed' (Fake) News." *USA Today*, 6 March 2017. http://www.usatoday.com/story/tech/news/2017/03/06/facebook-begins-flagging-disputed-fake-news/98804948.

Huppke, Rex. "It's Not Fake News, It's Web Dung." *Chicago Tribune*, 13 January 2017. http://www.chicagotribune.com/news/opinion/huppke/ct-fake-news-trump-huppke-20170113-story.html.

International Federation of Library Associations and Institutions. "How to Spot Fake News" (infographic), 18 November 2016. https://www.ifla.org/publications/node/11174.

Kiely, Eugene, and Lori Robertson. "How to Spot Fake News." *Factcheck.org*, 18 November 2016. http://www.factcheck.org/2016/11/how-to-spot-fake-news.

Kranich, Nancy. "Democracy Statement." American Library Association, 2016. http://www.ala.org/aboutala/governance/officers/past/kranich/demo/statement.

Liebmann, Larissa U. 2014. "Fraud and First Amendment Protections of False Speech: How United States v. Alvarez Impacts Constitutional Challenges to Ag-Gag Laws." *Pace Environmental Law Review* 31 (2014): 565.

Mackenzie, Catriona, and Natalie Stoljar. *Relational Autonomy: Feminist Perspectives on Autonomy, Agency, and the Social Self.* New York: Oxford University Press, 2000.

Madison, James. In Gaillard Hunt (ed.), *The writings of James Madison comprising his public papers and his private correspondence, including numerous letters and documents now for the first time printed*, Volume 9. New York: G. P. Putnam's Sons, 1910 (1822). http://press-pubs.uchicago.edu/founders/documents/v1ch18s35.html.

Meiklejohn, Alexander. *Free Speech and Its Relation to Self-Government.* New York: Harper, 1948.

Merriam-Webster. "News." Merriam-Webster.com, 2018. https://www
     .merriam-webster.com/dictionary/news.

Mill, John Stuart. *On Liberty*, Indianapolis: Hackett Publishing, 1978 (1859).

Ohlheiser, Abby. "This Is How Facebook's Fake-News Writers Make
     Money." *Washington Post*, 18 November 2016. https://www
     .washingtonpost.com/news/the-intersect/wp/2016/11/18/this-is
     -how-the-internets-fake-news-writers-make-money.

Parkinson, Hannah Jane. "Click and Elect: How Fake News Helped
     Donald Trump Win a Real Election." *The Guardian*, 14 Novem-
     ber 2016. https://www.theguardian.com/commentisfree/2016/nov
     /14/fake-news-donald-trump-election-alt-right-social-media-tech
     -companies.

Ranganathan, Siyali Ramamrita. *The Five Laws of Library Science.*
     Madras: The Madras Library Association, 1931.

Scanlon, Thomas. "A Theory of Freedom of Expression." *Philosophy and
     Public Affairs* 1, no. 2 (1972): 204–226.

Scott, Shane. "The Fake Americans Russia Used to Influence the Election."
     New York Times, 17 September 2017. https://www.nytimes.com/2017
     /09/07/us/politics/russia-facebook-twitter-election.html.

Shearer, Elisa, and Jeffrey Gottfried. "News Use across Social Media Plat-
     forms 2017." *Pew Research Center,* 17 September 2017. http://www
     .journalism.org/2017/09/07/news-use-across-social-media-platforms
     -2017/.

Silverman, Craig. "How the Bizarre Conspiracy Theory behind "Pizzagate"
     Was Spread." *Buzzfeed*, 4 November 2016a. https://www.buzzfeed
     .com/craigsilverman/fever-swamp-election.

Silverman, Craig. "This Analysis Shows How Viral Fake Election News
     Stories Outperformed Real News on Facebook." *Buzzfeed*, 16
     November 2016b. https://www.buzzfeed.com/craigsilverman/viral
     -fake-election-news-outperformed-real-news-on-facebook.

Silverman, Craig, and Jeremy Singer-Vine. 2016. "Most Americans Who
     See Fake News Believe It, New Survey Says." *Buzzfeed*, 6 Decem-
     ber 2016. https://www.buzzfeed.com/craigsilverman/fake-news
     -survey.

Snow, Jackie. "Can AI Win the War against Fake News?" *MIT Technology
     Review*, 13 December 2017. https://www.technologyreview.com/s
     /609717/can-ai-win-the-war-against-fake-news/.

Sydell, Laura. "We Tracked Down a Fake-News Creator in the Suburbs.
     Here's What We Learned." NPR, 23 November 2016. http://www

.npr.org/sections/alltechconsidered/2016/11/23/503146770/npr
-finds-the-head-of-a-covert-fake-news-operation-in-the-suburbs.

West, Darrell M. "How to Combat Fake News and Disinformation." *Brookings*, 18 December 2017. https://www.brookings.edu/research/how
-to-combat-fake-news-and-disinformation/.

West, Richard, Russell Meserve, and Keith Stanovich. "Cognitive Sophistication Does Not Attenuate the Bias Blind Spot." *Journal of Personality and Social Psychology* 103, no. 3 (2012): 506–519.

SEVEN

Truth, Post-Truth, and Information Literacy: Evaluating Sources

Joanna M. Burkhardt

> Teaching the evaluation of information is possible and necessary at all libraries for all age levels. Instilling the habit of critical thinking may be the only way to reliably overcome the many ways misinformation, disinformation, and malinformation can reach us.

Before the Internet, it was fairly easy to identify reliable scholarly sources of information written by experts in their fields. In university and college libraries, the card catalog provided access to books selected by subject specialists in the library. Those subject selectors chose books for library collections, paying careful attention to author credentials, publisher reputation, content, and reviews written by other experts. Paper indexes provided access to citations for articles published in scholarly journals with peer review and publisher reputation to safeguard the quality and veracity of the information. There was a fairly clear delineation between scholarly and popular publications.

Initially, computerization of the information from the card catalog and the journal indexes was very helpful. Computer networking allowed libraries to share information about their holdings more widely, making the location of research materials faster. The advent of the Internet made it possible for individuals to do their own information gathering from remote locations. When it became possible to share the full text of scholarly books and journal articles online, the possibilities for researchers expanded exponentially.

In the early days of the Internet, the government and institutions of higher education bore the costs for access to information accessed via the Internet. In the early 1990s, however, the government decided to step away from funding the Internet. This meant that a different business model was needed to support infrastructure, make improvements, and incorporate new options. At first, individuals wanting to mount their Web pages on the Internet paid for that privilege. Not long after, advertisers offset those costs by paying Web site owners to have products displayed on their Web pages. This change affected access to scholarly information drastically.

The invention of the World Wide Web made it possible to create and use Web pages without the need to know anything about programming, opening wide and democratizing input of and access to massive amounts of information. Suddenly anyone in any part of the world could access information that had formerly been unavailable or unobtainable. Likewise, anyone could post information about any subject. It certainly seemed that more information was better, more participation was better, more input was better. And, for a time, it was.

The lines that had formerly existed between scholarly expert information and popular nonexpert information became blurred on the Internet. It was hard to sift out scholarly information, not only because information on the Internet all looked pretty much the same but also because the large volume of information available made that process much more time-consuming. Yet knowing what information was scholarly and what was not was and is essential to the goals of higher education in general and of science in particular.

As participation in Internet use became global and search engines classified and categorized huge quantities of information, author credentials and expertise and publisher reputation took a backseat to the immediate gratification of getting information quickly. Tom Nichols describes the lack of concern about expertise as "a Google-fueled, Wikipedia-based, blog-sodden collapse of any division between professionals and laymen, students and teachers, knowers and wonderers—in other words, between those with any achievement in an area and those with none at all" (Nichols 2014).

For some time, instructors and librarians at institutions of higher education were vigilant in checking sources students cited for authority, and they were stringent about the kinds of sources they considered acceptable for academic work. However, the everyday practices of students searching for nonacademic information gradually bled into the academic world. The definitions of expertise and authority also became blurred as new kinds of information created by new kinds of authors began to appear. Was a blogger a reliable source? How did one find out? If a graduate degree in a field of higher education was no longer the determining credential for expertise, what was? These questions about authority further diluted the distinctions between popular and scholarly information.

Scholarly information is often locked up behind a paywall. People seeking information can access citations to information but cannot get the information itself without paying for it. Many institutions purchase expensive subscriptions to full-text online journals and other scholarly information and pass that access on to their constituents. If one happens to be affiliated with an institution providing such a service, one has access to the information. Once individuals are no longer constituents (as when students graduate from college), they no longer have access to scholarly information and usually revert back to information they can access for free.

Free and open access to some but not all information quickly returns us to a world of scholarly information haves and have-nots. While scholars at institutions of higher education go on about their business, potential scholars and those without the ability to pay for scholarly information are forced to rely on other often less accurate and less reliable sources of information. Because expert information is often hidden behind a paywall, people seeking information must rely on what is available to them for free, despite the fact that the information they find may not be accurate or reliable. Jane Devine and Francine Egger-Sider say students look for convenience of use and speed over accuracy when seeking information. They further state "when researchers use freely available sources, the order of use is Google, Google Scholar, Wikipedia and YouTube" (2014, p. 5).

This situation has continued to devolve as technological advances have appeared. Mobile computers, cell phones, wi-fi, and social media have made access to information available to billions of people around the world. Information can come from anyone and anywhere. It can be true; it can be false; it can be misleading. There is no easy process to sort out "good" information from "bad" information. Attempts to improve the situation (Open Access journals, for example) have been blemished by bad actors who use those improvements to line their pockets and/or to push questionable information forward as if it met the standards for scholarly research. Add to this the algorithms and bots driving decision making, micro targeting, and propagandizing for advertisers, politicians, and special interest groups, especially on social media platforms. Mountains of information are available, but finding accurate, reliable information is harder than ever.

Thanks to the democratization of the Internet, anyone can participate in providing information. Everyone assumes the guise of an expert on the Internet. That makes the information they provide seem equally believable. In fact, many people appear to believe information is true *because* it appears on the Internet. David J. Helfand (2017, p. 2), quoting Clarke, notes that "most people have no clue how the technology that envelops them works or what physical principles underlie its operation—it is, truly, "indistinguishable from magic."[1] "Thus, the "limits of plausibility" have vanished, and the "knowledge of the audience" is constructed from Facebook feeds, personal experience, and anecdote" (O'Neil 2016, p. 70).

MISINFORMATION, DISINFORMATION, AND MALINFORMATION

Throughout history, there are recorded incidents of misinformation (incorrect information given whether accidentally or on purpose), disinformation (information using only selective information to support one side of an argument), and malinformation (propaganda). However, technology makes it possible to disseminate these kinds of information around the globe to billions of people in seconds. The number of people reached and the speed of reaching them have never been greater. This means the possible damage that can be done with inaccurate or false information is much greater than ever before. Incidents of so-called fake news being disseminated have become rampant, and the result of the spread of this kind of information has had negative and often harmful repercussions worldwide. For example, a Twitter hack allowed an account from a trusted news source to be used to send out a message saying there had been an explosion at the White House and that the president had been injured. This caused a 143-point fall in the Dow Jones industrial average, which, in turn, caused markets around the world to react (Moore and Roberts 2013).

HOW DOES MISINFORMATION SPREAD?

In order to use popular, "free" computer applications, people willingly give up personal information. Computer algorithms make it possible to gather and analyze this data. It can then be subdivided, categorized, and sold to anyone interested in buying it. Cathy O'Neil says, "If it was true during the early dot-com days that 'nobody knows you're a dog,' it's the exact opposite today. We are ranked, categorized, and scored in hundreds of models, on the basis of our revealed preferences and patterns" (2016, p. 70). Manipulation of data can carve out groups with similar characteristics creating audiences to whom purveyors of information can direct their messages.

Social media platforms collect data about what individuals have clicked on, liked, and shared and whom they shared information with. This information can then be sorted into infinite categories and monetized by selling it to anyone who would like to send information to a specific group. This allows groups with like interests to be targeted to receive information they did not ask for, produced by individuals or groups with a vested interest in marketing information that may or may not be true, accurate, and/or reliable.

Social media platforms and search engines provide access to targeted populations who receive messages often without ever knowing why or how they were targeted to receive them. The cost of designing specific target groups is so small that it can be cost-effective to send thousands of messages to very small groups of people. Because those messages are not seen by others outside the group, there is no way to know what information is contained in them.

SHORT-TERM AND LONG-TERM MEMORY

According to Daniel Gilbert (1991), the human brain has two types of memory—short-term, or working, memory and long-term memory. The short-term memory holds small amounts of information for immediate use. For example, a telephone number that is used once is held in short-term memory, giving the caller just enough memory to dial. Once dialed, the number is usually discarded to make room for other temporary memory needs.

If one has the need to use the same information often, the information moves from short-term memory to long-term memory. For example, when learning to read, children begin with individual letters and sounds. They hold letters in short-term memory until repetition moves them to long-term memory. Once the letters are housed in the long-term memory, the child can then learn how to combine them, again starting in the short-term memory. Repetition of those combinations of letters moves them into long-term memory. Combinations of letters can then be called up from long-term memory to allow the learning of words. And so on with sentences and paragraphs.

When information is learned in multiple ways, it is stored in multiple places in the brain. For example, when learning the alphabet, children see what letters look like; they hear what sounds each letter makes; they associate the letters with pictures of objects whose names begin with that letter; they sing songs about the letters; and they practice forming the letters themselves on paper. Each of these activities helps to create a new pathway to a place in long-term memory. When called upon to recollect the information, there are several pathways in the brain from which it can be recalled. The more pathways that exist, the easier it is to recall the needed information.

Gilbert explains that in order for the brain to process new information, the short-term memory "accepts" new information (that is, at least temporarily, the brain believes new information is true) simply to be able to understand it. Even for information determined to be false, when remembering it later, the brain tends to remember it as true.

Gilbert further explains that repetition has a large role in moving information into long-term memory. The more often one hears something, the more solidly it is cemented in long-term memory, even if the information is false. Repeated information creates familiarity, and familiarity gives the impression of truth, which reinforces belief. (This is why politicians and advertisers repeat things over and over.)

Trying to correct misinformation is very difficult for two reasons. First, in explaining why some information is incorrect, it is usual to restate the original information. By repeating the incorrect original information, it becomes more firmly established in the memory as true, even though it is false. Second, firmly held beliefs are almost impervious to correction. Attempts to correct these beliefs cause people to reject the correction and to more firmly hold to what they already believe, even if what they believe is false.

According to Gilbert, all of this means that the default setting in the brain to temporarily assume that new information is true, coupled with information practices that supply information similar to what individuals already know and like, creates information silos where new, different, or opposing information does not enter. If you receive only misinformation or even if you just receive the misinformation first, it becomes much more difficult to unbelieve. When opposing information comes to light, it is easier to dismiss it rather than to reconcile it with a previously held belief.

BORN IN THE DIGITAL AGE

Millennials and Gen Y members are the first to have lived their entire lives in a computerized world. Most of them have always been surrounded by computers and computer technology. Most are familiar with the manipulation of hardware and software, often with multiple devices and multiple formats. This familiarity with technology does not, however, make them information experts. What familiarity has done is make them often impatient when information is not provided instantaneously. It has been my experience with this age group that they want to use tools they already know to find information. They are not particularly worried about the accuracy of the information they find. Most do not do a deep dive for information but only skim the surface of their subject. They do not spend much time thinking about where the information came from or why they should question its veracity.

Andrew D. Asher says, "Students . . . often treat their interactions with search tools as 'magical' experiences and accept research results uncritically" (Asher 2015, p. 140). He goes on to say, "Students assume the best sources are on the first page of results" (p. 145). These assumptions are not unique to teenagers and young adults; most adults hold them as well.

Younger people in particular often get their news from social media sources. An estimated 67 percent of Americans get at least some of their news on social media, according to a Pew Research poll (Shearer and Gottfried 2017). The practices of using algorithms and bots to search out information that is similar to what a user has already liked, clicked on, or shared and then delivering only that kind of content to the user creates a one-sided story and strengthens confirmation bias in users who get their information in this manner.

Google is by far the most popular search engine, yet most people who look for information do not understand how Google works, what its relevance ranking is based on, or how the algorithm might be interpreting their search request. Searchers tend to assume that the "best" information will rise to the top of the result list in a Google search, but this is often not the case:

> Combined with inadequate source evaluations, the practice of using simple search and utilizing only the first page of results means that students are de facto out-sourcing much of the evaluation process to the search algorithm itself by relying on the search tool's relevancy rankings to determine resources quality. (Asher 2015, p. 145)

Novices in a subject area tend to overestimate how much they know about that subject. They tend to treat the Internet as an extension of their brains. When they use information from the Internet, they tend to forget that they didn't already know the information they found. This gives them confidence that they know more than they actually do (Fisher, Goddu, and Keil 2015). This overconfidence, based on information that has not been critically evaluated, allows misinformation to spread.

HOW LIBRARIES CAN HELP

While the situation is not quite hopeless, there is much work to be done to make people aware of where information comes from and how it can be used or misused. Education and training need to start early in life and continue to occur frequently and consistently. Critical thinking about information plucked from a mountain of Google search results or delivered to the social media doorstep is key to gaining access to accurate, reliable, and trustworthy information. Critical thinking is a habit of mind that should be cultivated in children and reinforced throughout the life span.

A recent Pew survey indicated that 87 percent of Millennials and 74 percent of Baby Boomers said that the library "is a place that helps them find information that is trustworthy and reliable" (Geiger 2017). Fully 61 percent of those surveyed said that getting training on how to identify reliable information would help them in making decisions. Because libraries are viewed as places where people know they can learn to identify reliable information, we should take every opportunity to supply this training. Teaching the evaluation of information is possible and necessary at all libraries for all age levels. Instilling the habit of critical thinking may be the only way to reliably overcome the many ways misinformation, disinformation, and malinformation can reach us.

Learning theorists offer some insights as to how we might create lessons that will be remembered and utilized. Brown, Roediger, and MacDaniel (2014) say that people learn better when they have to work hard to master a concept or skill. They learn better and remember longer when they practice self-discovery rather than receiving information in a lecture setting. Hands-on experience helps to strengthen memory by adding a physical component. People learn and remember when starting from something they know that can then be compared by analogy to a new idea. People learn and remember what they learned better if they have opportunities to practice applying the new information in a variety of situations. Finally, people learn and remember better when they work in small groups (Brown et al. 2014). All of this information can guide instructors in creating lessons in evaluation.

Many do not understand why misinformation, disinformation, and fake news are a problem. To help them understand the problem, offer students a specific example of the spread of misinformation and its repercussions. It is not difficult to find examples that show how the spread of inaccurate material has had an effect on the local community or the world. The 2016 presidential campaign in the United States, the debunked research on vaccinations and autism, the "birther" movement regarding Barack Obama, and the Arab Spring communications—both individual and governmental—are examples that can be used to explain the means by which false or misleading information can be spread, as well as what the consequences are for the spread of that information.

Using tools that are familiar is important to making instruction relevant to students. By starting at a familiar place, instructors can meet students where they normally begin their search for information. Google is the go-to search engine for most students. It is familiar and easy to use. No matter what the subject, a search will return information. For these reasons, Google is a good starting place.

It is also useful to have students offer their own ideas about what criteria they would use to evaluate information for accuracy, reliability, and trustworthiness. By asking them to supply criteria, they engage in considering what might be important and relevant. Students can be encouraged to explain why they feel each criterion is important and what it might tell them about the information itself. The instructor can always ask questions or offer suggestions to fill in any gaps.

Once they have a list of evaluative criteria, students can perform a Google search for a current event or issue, for example, global warming. Ask them to consider the number of results they get. Ask the students to describe how the relevancy ranking in Google works. If they cannot do so, help them to understand why the sites that appear at the top of the list are not necessarily the sites that will provide the best information. Ask how many of the results they might reasonably be able to look at and what they might do to narrow their search to something more specific. Have the students describe how they would determine which results to look at and why.

Next, have the students apply their evaluation criteria to one item from the result list generated by a Google search. Their questions might include:

- What group is responsible for the information? Does the URL offer any information about the site?
- Is there a named author?
- What are the author's credentials? Does the author have a college degree, graduate degree, experience in the field, years of work at a reputable institution? What makes this person someone you would trust to give you reliable, accurate, and unbiased information?
- Does the Web site and/or the author say where their information comes from? Do they provide citations and links to reliable information sources?
- Do the citations and links connect, and do they connect to relevant information?
- If there is a picture with the story, right click on the picture and search for the picture in Google. Where does the picture come from? Is it related to the story? Is it connected with a different story?
- Is a reason given for why the information is being shared? Is there a mission statement for the organization that supports the Web site? Does that philosophy correspond with the information being offered?
- Is the information credible? Do citations and links back up the information offered? Is there a bibliography or list of further readings? (Students can adjust their opinions about this first link as they examine other links.)
- Is the content provided meant to evoke an emotional response? If so, what words, phrases, or images are used for this purpose?
- Is there advertising on the page? Is the Web site actively trying to sell something?
- Do the facts stand up under scrutiny at a fact-checking site such as FactCheck.com or Snopes.com?
- After answering these questions, is this information something you would consider accurate, reliable, unbiased, and truthful?

Students will quickly realize that evaluating even one Web site is time-consuming. They need to hear early and often that the evaluation of information is critical. Even though it is time-consuming, the selection of information that is accurate, reliable, and trustworthy will produce better results for decision making, for creating products and projects, and for being an informed citizen of the world.

Instructors can go on to introduce students to academic databases. Identifying the differences between Google and an academic database can help students to understand how they can get better results for research-related projects. However, because most databases supplied by academic institutions become unavailable to students once they have graduated, I would argue that learning how to evaluate information that is freely available to the general public is a higher-priority use of instruction time, when that time is limited.

It is worth pointing out that many employers list critical thinking as one of the top five skills they look for in new hires (Omoth 2017). They want to hire people who can find and evaluate information that can be applied to problems and projects in the workplace. For students who will be seeking employment in the near future, the ability to find and evaluate information will be an added credential for a resume and a valued skill in the workplace. This increases the relevance of the process.

CONCLUSION

Critical thinking applied to the evaluation of information is key to survival in a world where it is impossible to control misinformation, disinformation, and malinformation. This is a skill that is vital to everyone. Libraries are viewed as places where instruction in the discovery of accurate, reliable, and trustworthy information is available. Librarians should take advantage of this belief to provide as much instruction as possible, for every age level and in every type of library.

NOTE

1. This refers to Arthur C. Clarke's Third Law, which states, "Any technology, sufficiently advanced, is indistinguishable from magic" (Clarke 1974, p. 39).

REFERENCES

Asher, Andrew D. "Search Epistemology: Teaching Students about Information Discovery." In Troy A. Swanson and Heather Jagman (eds.), *Not Just Where to Click: Teaching Students How to Think about*

Information, 139–154. Chicago: Association of College & Research Libraries, 2015.

Brown, Peter C., Henry L. Roediger III, and Mark A. MacDaniel. *Make It Stick*. Cambridge, MA: Belknap Press of Harvard University, 2014.

Clarke, Arthur C. *Profiles of the Future: An Inquiry into the Limits of the Possible*. London: V. Gollancz, 1974.

Devine, Jane, and Francine Egger-Sider. *Going beyond Google Again: Strategies for Using and Teaching the Invisible Web*. Chicago: Neal Schuman, 2014.

Fisher, Matthew, Mariel K. Goddu, and Frank C. Keil. "Searching for Explanations: How the Internet Inflates Estimates of Internal Knowledge." *Journal of Experimental Psychology: General* 144, no. 3 (2015): 674–687.

Geiger, Abigail. "Most Americans—Especially Millennials—Say Libraries Can Help Them Find Reliable, Trustworthy Information." Pew Research Center, 30 August 2017. http://www.pewresearch.org/fact-tank/2017/08/30/most-americans-especially-millennials-say-libraries-can-help-them-find-reliable-trustworthy-information/.

Gilbert, Daniel T. "How Mental Systems Believe." *American Psychologist* 46, no. 2 (1991): 107–119.

Helfand, David J. "Surviving the Misinformation Age." *Skeptical Inquirer* 413 (May/June 2017). https://www.csicop.org/si/show/surviving_the_misinformation_age.

Moore, Heidi, and Dan Roberts. "AP Twitter Hack Causes Panic on Wall Street and Sends Dow Plunging." *The Guardian*, 23 April 2013. https://www.theguardian.com/business/2013/apr/23/ap-tweet-hack-wall-street-freefall.

Nichols, Thomas. 2014. "The Death of Expertise." The Federalist, 17 January 2014. http://thefederalist.com/2014/01/17/the-death-of-expertise.

Omoth, Tyler. "The Top 5 Job Skills That Employers Are Looking for in 2017." TopResume, n.d. https://www.topresume.com/career-advice/the-top-5-job-skills-that-employers-are-looking-for-in-2017.

O'Neil, Cathy. *Weapons of Math Destruction: How Big Data Increases Inequality and Threatens Our Democracy*. New York: Crown, 2016.

Shearer, Eliza, and Jeffrey Gottfried. "News Use across Social Media Platforms." Pew Research Center, 4 October 2017. http://www.pewresearch.org/fact-tank/2017/10/04/key-trends-in-social-and-digital-news-media/.

EIGHT

We Got This: Public Libraries as Defenders against Fake News

Ben Himmelfarb

Fake news may lose its "buzzword" status over time, but promoting information literacy and informed civil discourse will remain part of public libraries' missions for the foreseeable future.

WHY FAKE NEWS?

In the fall of 2016, before and after the U.S. presidential election, the phrase "fake news" was everywhere: headlines, tweets, chyrons, e-mail subject lines. A phrase that had been used to describe fringe or satirical content (i.e., the *National Enquirer*, *The Onion*) was suddenly being applied to previously unassailable sources of news, such as *The New York Times* and *The Washington Post*. Almost any story or report could be subjected to the slur, and sources that were once viewed as unbiased were suddenly attacked as partisan.

Some news users were less surprised than others by the transformation of public discourse. One's level of surprise was usually proportionate to the amount of time spent on the Internet. Ten years of explosive growth in social media use, the erosion of public trust in institutions, high levels of polarization between America's two most powerful political parties, and legitimate frustration with the slow and unequal pace of economic recovery since the 2008 financial crisis created the conditions for a disruptive election year. So in 2016, when the dog whistle was dropped in favor of easily heard frequencies, a system for delivering news to the public that had seemed stable was revealed to be precarious. Almost everyone had to adjust his or her thinking and ways of interpreting events that were deemed "news-worthy." It was traumatic. It was an opportunity.

WE OWN THIS

As a public library, we felt compelled to address the issue of fake news and information literacy for a few reasons. First, people were talking about it—at the reference desk, in staff offices, and during other library programs. Second, as a supplier of media (both mainstream and fringe), we felt it was part of our basic mission to assist people using our resources to access information. Third, the fake news issue touches on the core values that animate public libraries: intellectual freedom, equitable access to library and information services, literacy, and lifelong learning. The mission of White Plains Public Library specifically calls on us to offer "personal guidance" in the use of information resources and to provide "diverse opportunities for cultural exchange and exploration of ideas."

Even though "fake news" was a term with political implications and often sat at the core of people's views on the 2016 election, we believed there was room for nonpartisan, innovative, basically uncontroversial library programming. After all, every day we helped people determine the veracity of information and regularly offered guidance on the quality of different sources. We knew we could fulfill our public's desire to discuss and learn about fake news without taking sides or fomenting controversy.

DEVELOPING A WORKSHOP

Driving to work one morning in November, listening to *On the Media*'s podcast (*OTM*), I heard the radio hosts promote their *Breaking News Consumer's Handbook: Fake News Edition* (http://www.wnyc.org/story /breaking-news-consumer-handbook-fake-news-edition/). I was a fan of their earlier handbooks that offered guidance on how to interpret news about terrorist attacks or coverage of people experiencing poverty. *OTM* did solid work helping people discover the biases embedded in their news diets. They offered ways of processing information rationally, in spite of the hysterical tone of news anchors or frantic pace of developing stories (if you watch

CNN long enough, you'll realize that "BREAKING NEWS" banner is just up all the time). *OTM* was doing the work our mission called on us to do!

That morning, I figured I would just add *OTM*'s handbook to the list of things I could recommend to people who came to the library with questions about the news. I also printed a few copies for my coworkers. This began a conversation about the opportunity to create a program presented by the rise of fake news. With the support of library administration, I began to develop a public program.

INTO THE COMMUNITY

From the beginning, we wanted the workshop to take place outside the building, in the course of people's everyday lives. This was important to us because we wanted to reach beyond the people who were already coming to the library and who were possibly already engaged in some kind of critical relationship with the news. We wanted to reach people who visited the same limited Web sites every day and didn't know how to find new ones, as well as people who desired contact with people of different political persuasions because all of their friends shared their politics. We also wanted to reach people who literally never wondered whether the news was "true" before 2016. As many librarians can attest, 2016 made even experienced information professionals recognize the need to brush up on their media literacy skills.

I identified diverse groups within our community to approach about participating in workshops. Workshops were eventually held with a youth group for young women of color, a group of retired men, a current events discussion group that met in a diner, an adult education group based out of a synagogue, our local Rotary Club, and an organization that helped seniors maintain independence and integration in the community We also hosted two sessions in our library. Since the issue of fake news was persisting beyond election day, we did not feel it was urgent to squeeze in as many workshops as possible in a certain period of time. We were reassured by the perennial nature of fake news issues in the first months of 2017 that opportunities for engagement on this issue would persist. And we were not disappointed!

As with any workshop, I figured participants would benefit from a presentation at the beginning of the session, though I knew this was a topic that had to be talked about, had to be discussed. It was important to me that the workshop respect people's eagerness to speak on the issue. I didn't want to overplan, so I kept the presentation basic, and used the *OTM* handbook as an outline. The handbook, however, mostly focused on fake news as it pertained to Internet users. Because it was not geared toward print or radio news users, I drew parallels between the formats and brought the difference up as a topic of discussion. Terms like "reading" or "watching" the news often drew challenges from participants who did one but not the other. To avoid this semantic (but important) bump in the road, I started telling people I would use the term "news consumer" or "news user." This gave clarity to the discussion and introduced personal responsibility into the discussion.

WHAT HAPPENED

I began each workshop by taking a poll: What were people's main sources of news? As one would expect, younger people tended to rely more on the Internet, while older people watched more television news and read more print news. Within the Internet user groups, however, there were important distinctions. Some folks who had online subscriptions to mainstream sources like *The New York Times* or *The Washington Post* considered themselves primarily Internet-based news readers. The teens whom I asked about their Internet use mentioned platforms for sharing news rather than specific journalistic organizations. Answers like "Facebook," "Tumblr," "Snapchat," and "YouTube" were given. When pressed about the sources of the information they accessed through a given platform, the teens were less specific, though some realized that they were using mainstream sources without ever going to the actual site (i.e., they read excerpts from a *Washington Post* article someone posted as a status or relied on skimming the headlines on Twitter).

The slideshow I developed had a separate slide for each of the basic tips for spotting fake news on the Internet. I included popular examples to demonstrate each tip in action. There were slides for investigating suspicious domain names, using fact-checking sites, comparing headlines to the content of articles, and spotting common red flags like the use of all capital letters, manipulated images, and unsourced claims. I also created slides with relevant words like "truth," "post-truth," "objectivity," "bias," and "news," accompanied by their definitions. Some basic etymological information from the *Oxford English Dictionary* aided discussion. These slides focused conversation because they helped participants to become more exact in their language and not talk past one another.

Fears of conflict or controversy derailing the program on our part were minimal. We knew the groups we were going to work with well; the library had a strong reputation within the community as a trustworthy resource, and we were not pushing a partisan perspective. The presentation included examples of fake news used in the service of liberal and conservative agendas. Rather than just getting people into a room and letting them "have at it," we developed discussion questions aimed beyond partisanship. Some examples:

- How do we use the individual power we have to learn, seek, discern, and find the truth?
- Most of us have a few sources we rely on for news (this is okay—we all can't read everything). What are some of yours?
- How do you try to balance your news diet—if you do?
- When was the last time you had your mind changed on an issue?
- Do you have friends or family that you disagree with politically but manage to talk to or maintain a relationship with?
- Have you ever shared an article or video online without reading or watching it first?
- How do you feel after spending time on Facebook or Twitter? After watching news programs on television? After reading a long-form article in a magazine?
- How often do you verify stories (either by fact-checking or by waiting for corroboration from other sources)?
- How do you tell the difference between fake, false, or unfair news?

Presenting open-ended questions that people of all political backgrounds could answer was key to facilitating healthy, respectful conversations. Most people were much more interested in these types of questions than in debates about the story du jour. It was enlightening to see people with differing political views commiserate over the challenges of navigating the world of fake (and real) news.

WHAT THEY LEARNED

I relied on informal conversations and unsolicited feedback to evaluate the effect of the program. Participants routinely experienced revelations based on talking with one another or applying the knowledge from our presentation. One high schooler said she used YouTube to watch raw video because it was closer to what actually happened, but she also knew that it wasn't the whole story and that she would have to find journalism that gave her background. A woman in her 60s at the current events discussion group in the diner realized for the first time that her online news aggregator page was not the same as everyone else's—that it was curated by an algorithm—when she compared what was on her news app with the headlines displayed on her neighbor's phone.

In one of the most powerful moments from the workshops, a group of seniors in an adult education class at a synagogue received a stern admonition from one of their own. Frustrated by her friends' desire for someone to tell them what they could trust, a participant admonished them to not rely on others and to seek out the truth for themselves. She felt that if we were passive consumers of news, we were apt to be manipulated and made narrow-minded. With that succinct, information-literacy–esque comment, she created unity among a group that often engaged in heated debates during their meetings.

Perhaps unsurprisingly, a generational divide between younger and older participants emerged during the workshops. In general, younger people were more skeptical and cynical, questioning the veracity of news from any source, whether it be *The New York Times* or an activist's Twitter feed. While some younger people cleaved to alternative news sources like YouTube commentators or activist groups, others acknowledged that mainstream sources had plenty of reliable information, just not *all* of the information. There was no question, for them, about the importance of challenging any source that claimed a monopoly on truth. Older people (again, in general) were more upset by the topsy-turvy world of competing news sources. Countless people cited Walter Cronkite as an example of unbiased reporting and asserted that monolithic, pre-Internet sources of information were more reliable.

Outright conflict during the workshops was rare. While our sample size is obviously small, liberals and conservatives were represented in workshops. And, more importantly, people often discussed the way specific news issues were covered rather than focusing on conventional partisan talking points. One participant felt *The New York Times* was reliably unbiased in its domestic political reporting but felt the paper was too pro-Palestinian. Another participant countered that *The Times*'s reporting on Palestine was something she appreciated but felt their political reporting was too conservative. These two participants agreed -to disagree, but both also acknowledged the areas where they could expand their news diets to include additional sources. Rather than just extending the seemingly endless debates highlighted on cable news, participants were encouraged to take a step back and engage in self-reflection in a safe, communal setting. In this way, we avoided offering tacit support for a particular perspective and promoted public libraries' capacity for self-directed, lifelong learning.

Since this was, after all, a library program, it wouldn't have been complete without some hostile interrogation of the librarian. Deep into a conversation on the nature of truth, a participant asked me, "Well, would the library put the *National Enquirer* on the shelf next to *The New Yorker* and *The Economist*? I mean, you can't really do that, can you?"

I, along with everyone else, laughed. My answer was probably not what she expected. I told her that we have a collections policy that dictates what we purchase. If there was sufficient demand for it, we would buy it, and it would be located with other periodicals.

"But what if someone picked it up and read that Hillary Clinton had an alien baby? What would you tell them if they told you that?" she asked.

I told her I would go through the same process with that person that I would with anyone who asked me to help them verify a story. We could look for corroboration in other publications. If we found none, we'd look to the article itself and see whether it mentioned sources. We would repeat the process in additional publications until we reached a reasonable conclusion about the veracity of the story. When she continued, incredulous, that the *National Enquirer* was "pure fiction!" I replied that we also had a section for that.

WHAT WE LEARNED

Workshop participants eventually turned to answering the question, "So what do we do after we leave this program?" The workshop itself was often cited as a healthy response to current conditions. People felt overwhelmed by the volume of news and information in the world. Even if you tried to limit your exposure, participants often said, that meant you might miss something or fall prey to the dreaded "echo chamber." While it is not librarians' job to make people feel "good" based on the information we provide, this was clearly a situation when guidance and companionship would do just that. People felt relieved to have other human beings to talk to, in person, rather than scrolling alone through vitriolic comment threads.

People wanted help becoming savvy, 21st-century news users. While many participants lauded the ability of having more people to create, access, and share information through the Internet, many felt things were better before we had so many options. Others countered with a critique of the pre-Internet information culture as too tightly controlled by hegemonic economic and political forces. It was proper, in their view, that there is more responsibility on people seeking truth now. When you could just turn on the six o'clock news and get the "truth," they said, it was easier to be fooled, and you were less likely to question the authority of the few sources that existed.

The lessons we learned through our work are interwoven with our narrative. However, to summarize:

- People wanted to talk about fake news, and they wanted to do it together.
- There was no push-back at all about our library offering programming on this topic.
- Most people were relieved to step away from debating the veracity of specific stories.
- People were eager to give their time and attention to constructive dialogue.
- We did not overplan the program—we balanced a prepared presentation with a large stock of discussion questions and flexible facilitation.
- Our main goal was to strengthen people's information literacy skills, but we also improved their relationship to the library and library staff.
- Taking programs outside the library helped us reach people who weren't coming to the library and put information literacy education into the context of people's everyday lives, even people who did not identify as regular library users.
- A workshop on a very live issue expanded people's understanding of what libraries do, showing that we do not just work to preserve already recorded information but to serve as information educators for the community.

WHAT'S NEXT?

Librarians who want to do something about this issue are encouraged to first identify ways they are already dealing with fake news in their everyday work. Do you get questions at the reference desk about news stories?

Or unsolicited political comments from patrons? Has the issue bled into other programs you offer? If you see a desire for programming about fake news in your community, collect some of the basic, popular resources that have been developed. *On the Media*[1] has all of their handbooks online, and Melissa Zimdars's GoogleDoc[2] that started it all remains live as of October 2017.

Even with all of the great resources out there, don't overplan! Put together some helpful, relevant materials, then contact community groups and make your pitch. Make sure to leave plenty of space for participants to help determine the content of the workshop.

Fake news may lose its buzzword status over time, but promoting information literacy and informed civil discourse will remain part of public libraries' missions for the foreseeable future. The biggest question that this workshop raised for us is still unanswered. How can we, as a public library, engage with relevant, possibly controversial issues from an informational perspective? For instance, is there a need for a workshop on the community planning process or on national health care debates? And, if there is, how do we connect people with good information without wading into political controversy? Our experience creating and hosting fake news workshops gives us hope that we have valuable expertise to offer and that the public might desire it more than even we know.

NOTES

1. All of *On the Media*'s *Breaking News Consumer's Handbook*s are available online at https://www.wnycstudios.org/shows/otm/handbooks.

2. Professor Melissa Zimdars's original GoogleDoc is viewable at https://docs.google.com/document/d/10eA5-mCZLSS4MQY5QGb5ewC3VAL6pLkT53V_81ZyitM/preview. She has also started a site (www.opensources.co) that is a professionally curated lists of online sources, available for public use for free.

NINE

School Librarians: Partners in the Fight against Fake News

Kristen Mattson

The notion that students are digital natives, born into a world with technology that adults have had to migrate into, reinforces some teachers' fears that their students may know more about the digital devices in the classroom than they will. What many adults fail to realize is that young people's online experiences are typically centered on socialization and entertainment.

INTRODUCTION

Public schools are changing, and school librarianship is changing along with them. In the not too distant past, the school library was the hub of all student inquiry and research assignments, and the librarian was often the gatekeeper between low-quality information and the students. Today, however, students and teachers are accessing information more readily from the classroom thanks to increased mobile technologies, more robust wireless Internet access, and the trend in school libraries to purchase fewer nonfiction print materials in favor of online database subscriptions that can be utilized both on and off campus. While increased access to information is certainly something that librarians celebrate, the downside is that students are engaging in research and inquiry tasks without the guidance and support of an expert who can teach the skills needed to do so effectively.

In a time when the whole country seems to be talking about fake news, standards of journalism, the easy spread of misinformation, and the distortion of fact to fit a prescribed narrative, an ironically unfortunate trend is also happening in school districts around the country. As many schools adopt digital devices and online curricular materials, putting their students in the middle of an information storm, they are also opting to eliminate their school librarians in favor of low-paid, noncertified staff who can manage the reduced print collections. Savings are typically spent to hire technology coaches who can support teachers with the ins and outs of particular devices and platforms (Boudrye 2014). In this rapidly changing environment, school boards have failed to realize that there is a more pressing need for certified school librarians than ever before.

Interestingly enough, school districts that have chosen to keep their certified teacher librarians have actually had an easier time transitioning their staff and students to learning environments whereby technology and, in turn, access to all sorts of information are much more ubiquitous. In many cases, school librarians are leading the charge in a changing landscape of instructional design, student-centered learning, digital reading, writing, and note taking, as well as the myriad of skills related to information and media literacy (Wolf, Jones, and Gilbert 2014).

This chapter will outline the tensions between the need for more media and information literacy education in classrooms and the current realities in K–12 schools. It will also shine a light on the opportunities that school librarians have to come alongside classroom teachers as curriculum developers, coteachers, and even instructional coaches to more seamlessly integrate the skills related to information and media literacy, the weapons in the battle against fake news, into traditional areas of the K–12 curriculum.

FAKE NEWS AND CRITICAL THINKING

A 2016 study from the Stanford Graduate School of Education assessed the abilities of more than 7,800 middle, high school, and college-level students to evaluate information presented online through various platforms and mediums. The researchers were appalled at the results, most notably that middle schoolers could not tell the difference between paid advertisements and actual articles, that most high schoolers accepted photographs and captions at face value without questioning their origins, and that most college students did not recognize the bias in facts presented by activist groups online (Stanford History Education Group 2016).

The fight against fake news begins with one's ability to think critically about the information in front of them. The importance of critical thinking as a required skill set has been emphasized by educational organizations and in numerous sets of student learning standards, including:

- The Common Core State Standards for English Language Arts/Literacy, which assert that students who are college and career ready must be "engaged and open-minded—but discerning—readers and listeners. They [must] work diligently to understand precisely what an author or speaker is saying, but they (should) also question an author's or speaker's assumptions and premises and assess the veracity of claims and the soundness of reasoning" (National Governors Association Center for Best Practices 2010).

- The College, Career and Civic Life (C3) Framework for social studies education, which emphasizes the need for students not only to critique the claims and evidence presented by others but also to develop sound arguments supported by relevant evidence and reasoning themselves (National Council for the Social Studies 2013).

- The International Society for Technology in Education's Standards for Students (2017, section 3b), which specifically state, students must be able to "evaluate the accuracy, perspective, credibility and relevance of information, media, data or other resources."

Essentially, the modern humanities curriculum paints an image of citizens who are in constant pursuit of learning and knowledge, who form questions about the world around them, who successfully seek out information from varied viewpoints, and who use that information to deepen their understanding, support argumentation, and refute unwarranted claims. Schools are no longer tasked with teaching children *what to think* but have been sent forth with a mission for teaching them *how to think*. So why did the students who participated in the Stanford study have such a difficult time discerning fact from fiction and being skeptical of the gray areas in between? Even though the course has been charted, the lead author on the study, Sam Wineburg, posits that "U.S. classrooms haven't caught up to the way information is influencing kids daily" (Domonoske 2016). His observation begs the question: Why haven't U.S. classrooms caught up, and who is helping teachers make these instructional shifts in practice?

WHY CAN'T CLASSROOMS CATCH UP?

If the whole country is talking about the fake news epidemic, what is stopping teachers from addressing this issue with gusto? Well, if one thing is true about education today, it is that rapid changes in curricular expectations, state and national standards, and accountability measures, as well as a steady rise in new technologies in the classroom, have left teachers feeling overwhelmed, overworked, and underprepared for all they've been asked to do.

As teachers have been encouraged to move away from teacher-centered, content-based learning and toward learning that is inquiry based and student centered and that requires engagement in various levels of critical thinking, there has been a simultaneous rise of both spending on and interest in the latest technology tools for education (Schaffhauser 2016). As online learning, blended learning, personalized learning, and inquiry-based learning become less the exception and more the rule, there has been an increase in professional development around such topics. Unfortunately, most of the learning and ongoing support for teachers is focused on how to navigate and use the various technology tools and platforms at their disposal rather than on the deeper issues and skills that are most concerning to information and media literacy educators (Hobbs and Jensen 2009), such as a person's ability to efficiently and effectively locate, evaluate, analyze, and use the information they find for specific purposes.

While many educators see the value in and importance of teaching these new literacy skills over the intricacies of a particular tool, both media and information literacy compete for time in the classroom with content-specific goals, students' social and emotional needs, technological literacy, and digital citizenship lessons (Hobbs and Jensen 2009). Also, very few teachers are specifically trained in and expected to teach information literacy skills as part of their written curriculum. Educators who are not specifically tasked with the job often feel that they do not have time in their curriculum to incorporate media and information literacy lessons into their day (Scheibe 2009), often leaving information professionals, such as the school librarian, scrambling to haphazardly fill learning gaps in ways that are usually reactive rather than proactive.

In addition to being pressed for time, teachers (like many other adults) are guilty of buying into the myth of the digital native (Wineberg and McGrew 2016). The notion that students are digital natives, born into a world with technology that adults have had to migrate into, reinforces the fear teachers have that their students may know more about the digital devices in the classroom than they will. What many adults fail to realize is that young people's online experiences are typically centered on socialization and entertainment. When students use digital tools for peer-to-peer interactions, they are referring to a completely different set of behaviors than an adult who uses the Internet for work or learning (Hobbs and Jensen 2009). As a result of these misconceptions, adults may avoid using technology in the classroom altogether, fail to address information and media literacy skills even as they assign projects that require students to use them, or assume there is no need to provide direct instruction on digital habits that can benefit students as lifelong learners.

Finally, practicing teachers may themselves lack the media and information skills that are needed to incorporate such lessons into the classroom. Many teacher preparation programs and accreditation bodies, such as the CAEP (Council for the Accreditation of Educator Preparation), have standards that emphasize traditional subject area knowledge over critical thinking skills, even today. Because terminology around media and information literacy are only alluded to and not listed explicitly in the Common Core and C3 Standards, they have still not made their way into the mainstream teacher educator programs (Meehan, Ray, Walker, and Schwarz 2015).

So while a need for critical thinking and sound information literacy skills is paramount in the fight against fake news, teachers have been ill equipped to fight the battle alone, as they wrestle with rapid changes to curricular expectations, the inundation of educational technology in the classroom, and an insufficient amount of professional learning on the topic. The desire by some teachers, parents, and administrators to hang onto traditional parts of the school curriculum, coupled with the pressure put on schools to instruct students in inquiry, critical thinking, and the use of research-based evidence to develop and support claims have created a tension of sorts that is being negotiated in classrooms around the country each and every day.

SCHOOL LIBRARIANS: NATURAL LEADERS IN A DIGITAL AGE

It is clear that schools must modify their approaches to teaching and learning in order to support students who are navigating a constantly evolving information landscape riddled with misinformation, corporate agendas, and biased viewpoints. However, the same decision makers who are often responsible for increased spending on technology initiatives in schools lack background knowledge in the intricacies of media and information literacy, both as stand-alone areas of study and as skills that can and should be integrated throughout the curriculum. Unfortunately, school administrators' knowledge of both educational technology and information literacy can be hindered by a lack of course offerings or licensing requirements for principal preparation (Mahoney and Khwaja 2016). And yet teachers look to these same leaders to set the conditions for the successful integration of such skills in the curricula.

Organizations and corporations that have long championed school librarianship are recognizing the building tension between increased spending on instructional technology and a hesitancy to upend the traditional school curricula in order to try something new. These groups are now working hard to help school boards, superintendents, and building principals develop a vision for digital age learning and understand the important role school librarians play in supporting teachers and students with the information skills they need today.

Follett School Solutions' *Project Connect* has the goal of educating superintendents on how to empower and utilize their school librarians as instructional partners and collaborative leaders. *Project Connect* partners attend educational conferences nationwide to share videos, documentaries, case studies, and white papers that highlight some of the country's most successful school librarians who are coming alongside teachers and administrators to help bring about change (Hubing 2015). With a similar goal, the Alliance for Excellent Education, a nonprofit, bipartisan advocacy and policy organization based out of Washington, D.C., recently launched its *Future Ready Schools* initiative. The initiative is intended to help K–12 school leaders maximize their efforts in integrating digital learning opportunities, as well as personalized, student-centered learning opportunities, into their organizations with a focus on helping students be ready for college, career, and citizenship (Alliance for Excellent Education 2016). Part of the *Future Ready Schools* initiative is a *Future Ready Librarian* framework, intended to help all stakeholders in education see the direct alignment between the skills of school librarians and the mission and vision of student learning in a digital age.

The good news is that the work of these groups, along with the collective efforts of school library organizations, seems to be paying off. In many places around the country, district and school administrators are looking to school librarians to lead the difficult work of authentically integrating digital tools and media and information literacy skills not only into the curriculum but into classrooms and professional development as well. Superintendents like Pam Moran (Virginia), Mat McRae (Michigan),

Timothy Purnell (New Jersey), and Karen Sullivan (Illinois) are publicly expressing their excitement about librarians as change agents in an evolving educational landscape (Miller 2016). These same superintendents advise their colleagues to embrace school librarians as instructional partners in the classroom, as models for other educators, and as connectors between students, teachers, the community, and the administration (Miller 2016).

Because "information literacy is the horizontal curriculum that underscores every content area" (Boudrye 2014, p. 56), librarians are the ideal candidate for the type of grassroots leadership it can take to influence curricular and pedagogical change in a school community. Librarianship is and must be transdisciplinary. A certified teacher librarian must know and understand a variety of vocabularies, disciplines, patrons, and information types in order to help teachers and their students locate, evaluate, and utilize the best resources for the inquiry task at hand (Filbert 2016). Librarians, because of their unique position in the school community, have the ability to support teachers of all skill levels with a variety of resources and professional supports. Rather than an authoritative figure who is "forcing" change or evaluating a teacher's performance, the school librarian can be a partner to come alongside a teacher, helping that teacher feel safe enough to take a risk, which in turn can usher in change.

PRACTICAL ADVICE FOR SCHOOL LIBRARIANS

School librarians have the responsibility of being information leaders in their organizations. In a constantly changing information landscape, this means that the school librarian must be a lifelong learner and should be keeping up with the latest in media and information literacy education. School librarians should have a knowledge base that includes:

- *A solid understanding of the differences between information and media literacy as well as how news literacy straddles both.* The News Literacy Project has a fabulous online platform called the Checkology Virtual Classroom. Its 12 core lessons, which take a total of about 20 hours to complete, were written for high school students but can be an excellent resource for teachers or librarians who also need to brush up on their own news literacy skills.

- *An understanding of fake news that goes beyond black and white.* News is presented in shades of gray and can be misleading in many ways. Read up on bias, pseudoscience, clickbait, misinformation, false attribution, propaganda, and doctored content. EAVI (European Association for Viewers Interests), a nonprofit organization based out of Brussels that advocates for media literacy as a vital component for full participation in civic life, has an excellent collection of free, online resources to help school librarians deepen their own understanding of the varied ways news can be manipulated.

- *A familiarity with the standards and principles related to media literacy education.* The National Association for Media Literacy Education (NAMLE) produced a document in 2007 called Core Principles of Media Literacy Education in the United States. These belief statements and goals for media literacy can be an excellent resource for librarians to assess their own depth of understanding about key concept, as well as to use as a crosswalk with content-specific standards during lesson planning and curriculum review or development.

With a strong foundation in media and information literacy to share, the school librarian will need to become just as comfortable instructing adults as instructing students. There are many ways, both formal and informal, that school librarians can serve as instructional partners, helping to integrate the lessons and skills students need to fight fake news and misinformation into the traditional curriculum. There are many models by which this type of work can happen, and librarians must often be flexible enough to work within each of them when the time calls for it.

Curriculum writing. In many organizations, the school library curriculum is written in isolation from any other content area. Librarians should express interest in modifying this approach and ask to sit in on the next building or district-wide subject-area curriculum review cycle. This approach has worked well for middle school librarians in Indian Prairie School District 204, who actively participated in a rewrite of the 6th-, 7th-, and 8th-grade social studies curriculum. As teachers and librarians collaborate on the essential questions of each course and the enduring understandings that students should have, they located natural places to help students learn the inquiry and information literacy skills that will serve them well both within and outside school (Davenport and Mattson 2018).

Professional learning communities. Professional learning communities (PLCs) are teams of either grade-level–alike or subject-area–alike teachers who meet on a regular basis to examine student learning, instructional practices, interventions and supports (DuFour and Eaker 2009). While some school librarians choose to engage in PLCs with other librarians in their district or region, another option is for the school librarian to sit in on several meetings with a teacher team in his or her building. By attending meetings on a regular basis, the librarian can listen for opportunities to embed information literacy skills into the work that is already being done in the classroom. The librarian can help identify gaps in instruction and offer to locate or create materials that can help support student learning.

Formal professional development. The American Association of School Librarians recently updated their position statement on the Instructional Role of School Librarians (2017). Not only does the statement describe the vital role that school librarians play in supporting student learning, but it also underscores the importance of the librarian as a teacher to fellow educators, administrators, and staff and specifically mentions formal professional development as one avenue by which to do so. These opportunities can be the perfect time to help all teachers develop a common vocabulary for information literacy, allow them to engage in Web evaluation tasks that they can replicate in their own classrooms, and help them tease out and recognize the embedded information literacy tasks that are in the projects they assign.

Guest teaching. Some teachers may see a need for information literacy lessons in their classroom but may not yet feel comfortable enough to teach them. As a guest teacher in the classroom, the school librarian can support students while simultaneously increasing the knowledge and toolbox of the classroom teacher. School librarians can encourage professional learning by asking the classroom teacher to stay and listen to the lesson and to provide feedback on how students reacted to new learning. They may also encourage teachers to observe for learning gaps that may need to be addressed in follow-up lessons.

One-on-one coaching. At times, a school librarian may have the desire to work with large groups or even the whole staff but, for whatever reason, may not have the opportunity to do so. The good news is that it takes only one teacher who is willing to collaborate to start making change happen. School librarians can offer to partner with a student teacher or new teacher who may be feeling overwhelmed or a veteran teacher who is looking for new ideas to liven up the classroom. When the librarian partners with a single teacher to collaboratively develop lessons, coteach, and reflect together on the process, it not only benefits the students and the teacher, but the success can lead to collaborations with more teachers as word spreads.

CONCLUSION

School librarians can no longer do their work alone, nor can they continue to keep their skills and talents to themselves. The proliferation of digital devices and the immediate access to the information they provide mean that all citizens, not just information specialists, must have the skills to locate, evaluate, and effectively use information. School librarians can build coalitions of adults with the knowledge and tools to fight fake news by sharing their knowledge and offering to support classroom teachers so that they may, in turn, support the students in their classrooms.

REFERENCES

Alliance for Excellent Education. "Future Ready Schools Announces New Project to Recognize School Librarians as Leaders in School Transformation," 24 June 2016. https://all4ed.org/press/future-ready -schools-announces-new-project-to-recognize-school-librarians-as -leaders-in-school-transformation/.

Boudrye, Jennifer. "What's in a Name?" *Teacher Librarian* 42, no. 1 (2014): 56–57.

Davenport, Allan, and Kristen Mattson. "Collaborative Leadership as a Catalyst for Change." *Knowledge Quest* 46, no. 3 (2018): 14–21.

Domonoske, Camila. "Students Have 'Dismaying' Inability to Tell Fake News from Real, Study Finds." NPR, 23 November 2016. https:// www.npr.org/sections/thetwo-way/2016/11/23/503129818/study -finds-students-have-dismaying-inability-to-tell-fake-news-from -real.

DuFour, Richard, and Robert Eaker. *Professional Learning Communities at Work: Best Practices for Enhancing Student Achievement.* Bloomington, IN: Solution Tree Press, 2009.

Filbert, Nathan W. "Framing the Framework: The Rigorous Responsibilities of Library and Information Science." *Reference & User Services Quarterly* 55, no. 3 (2016): 199–202.

Hobbs, Renee, and Amy Jensen. "The Past, Present, and Future of Media Literacy Education." *Journal of Media Literacy Education* 1, no. 1 (2009): 1.

Hubing, Kristin C. "Project Connect Promotes the School Librarian's Vital Role." AASA, May 2015. http://www.aasa.org/content.aspx ?id=37172.

Mahoney, Kerrigan R., and Tehmina Khwaja. "Living and Leading in a Digital Age: A Narrative Study of the Attitudes and Perceptions of School Leaders about Media Literacy." *Journal of Media Literacy Education* 8, no. 2 (2016): 77–98.

Meehan, Jessica, Brandi Ray, Amada Walker, Sunny Wells, and Gretchen Schwarz. "Media Literacy in Teacher Education: A Good Fit across the Curriculum." *Journal of Media Literacy Education* 7, no. 2 (2015): 81–86.

Miller, Rebecca T. "These Superintendents Are Sold on Libraries: Editorial." *School Library Journal*, 22 November 2016. http://www.slj.com/2016/11/opinion/editorial/these-superintendents-are-sold-on-libraries-editorial/.

National Association for Media Literacy Education. "Core Principles of Media Literacy Education in the United States," 2007. https://namle.net/publications/core-principles.

National Council for the Social Studies (NCSS). *The College, Career, and Civic Life (C3) Framework for Social Studies State Standards: Guidance for Enhancing the Rigor of K–12 Civics, Economics, Geography, and History.* Silver Spring, MD: NCSS, 2013.

National Governors Association Center for Best Practices, Council of Chief State School Officers. *Common Core State Standards for English Language Arts/Literacy.* Washington, DC: National Governors Association Center for Best Practices, Council of Chief State School Officers, 2010.

Schaffhauser, Dian. "Report: Education Tech Spending on the Rise. *THE Journal*, 19 January 2016. https://thejournal.com/articles/2016/01/19/report-education-tech-spending-on-the-rise.aspx.

Scheibe, Cynthia. "'Sounds Great, But I Don't Have Time!' Helping Teachers Meet Their Goals and Needs." *Journal of Media Literacy Education* 1, no. 1 (2009).

Stanford History Education Group. "Evaluating Information: The Cornerstone of Civic Online Reasoning," 22 November 2016.https://stacks.stanford.edu/file/druid:fv751yt5934/SHEG%20Evaluating%20Information%20Online.pdf.

Wineberg, Sam, and Sarah McGrew. "Why Students Can't Google Their Way to the Truth." *Education Week*, 1 November 2016.https://www.edweek.org/ew/articles/2016/11/02/why-students-cant-google-their-way-to.html.

Wolf, Mary Ann, Rachel Jones, and Daniel Gilbert. "Leading In and Beyond the Library." Alliance for Excellent Education, January 2014. https://all4ed.org/wp-content/uploads/2014/01/BeyondTheLibrary.pdf.

TEN

Information and Media Literacy Education: The Role of School Libraries

Belinha De Abreu

> In the end, the role of the future educator will be to help students understand and interpret the media.

In the past two years, we have had two new words introduced to dictionaries: "post-truth," which became the *Oxford English Dictionary*'s word of the year in 2016, and "fake news," which became the *Collins English Dictionary*'s word of the year 2017 (BBC News 2016; Flood 2017). Just the mere fact that these two words have received such high levels of publicity and have been legitimized in respected venues bridges the conversation about the importance and value of media and information literacy as a foundation to the work of school libraries and school library media specialists.

Oddly enough, both words prove to be a source of contention as well. They are a symptom of a growing lack of literacy among the general public. How can one claim "news" to be fake, if it is in fact "news"? That is where the source of contention arises. The past several years have given us an opportunity to see where a lack of guidance in evaluation of information, or of even thinking more deeply about how information is created, has led to an abyss where information overload exists without much discernment. A big criticism of the 2016 U.S. presidential election was in part due to information overload, but it had more to do with how information is read, misread, or even ignored.

Media literacy is defined as the ability to access, analyze, evaluate, communicate, and produce information in a variety of forms and formats (Thoman and Jolls, 2003). Instructing using media literacy offers opportunities for students to engage in a variety of texts, while asking them to critically consider how a message is conceived, the motive behind the message, and whether more than one perspective is possible or is viewed differently by various demographic groups such as individuals of another race, religion, or socioeconomic status.

Twenty-first-century learning requires teachers and students to design a partnership in which the flow of information can exist with the knowledge that technology is ever changing. The American Association of School Librarians (AASL) has been seeking to promote these skills through their definition of information literacy. It was expanded further as "a transformational process in which the learner needs to find, understand, evaluate, and use information in various forms to create for personal, social, or global purposes" (Abilock, 2004, p.10). AASL broadens the definition through their revised framework under the *INQUIRE* domain, which states, "Build new knowledge by inquiring, thinking critically, identifying problems, and developing strategies for solving problems" (American Association of School Librarians 2018, n.p.). Students need to be better viewers, seekers, and evaluators of ideas and information. Similar to media literacy, information literacy asks students to question common perceptions and to push information analysis further through investigation, evaluation, and discernment from various platforms, databases, resources, and applications.

READ

Providing students with multiple sources of information is something that school librarians strive to do. It is a beginning point for most research and allows multiple perspectives to be utilized. This is a key concept for media and information literacy. It addresses the questions, "Who is omitted from the message?" and "How might others interpret this message differently than I would?"

Most often, students do not consider the direction of the source for the information presented to them, especially when they are looking at it on the Internet. At the 2017 Family Online Safety Institute (FOSI) conference, a researcher mentioned that students are being more careful about passing on information, but the reality is that most students are not reading information thoroughly enough to make that determination. With all the movement and change in education in the past 15 years, the learning gap has also increased because, as educators, we are contextualizing print reading as similar to online reading. The two, however, differ in some important ways.

Reading online requires a different level of engagement. It is not linear but multilevel. The reader isn't going from left to right but up and down, sometimes to various components on a page. Reading online may even require a certain level of patience as the information sought isn't always so obvious. Students expect that relevant information will jump off an online page, but that doesn't often happen. It may require that students go through several pages, click on various links, and follow up on multiple pieces of information. This is where the school library media specialist can assist— in teaching students how to reach the critical depth of understanding that helps them validate information and not just seek it out. The students who claim "I can't find anything" when researching information online are mostly frustrated because they don't know how to process the amount of information that is presented to them.

MISREAD

"It is the job of the Fourth Estate [the media] to act as a check and a restraint on the others, to illumine the dark corners of Ministries, to debunk the bureaucrat, to throw often unwelcome light on the measures and motives of our rulers. *"News,"* as Hearst once remarked, *"is something which somebody wants suppressed: all the rest is advertising."* That job is an essential one, and it is bound to be unpopular; indeed, in a democracy, it may be argued that the more unpopular the newspapers are with the politicians, the better they are performing their most vital task" (Roberts 1955).

This brings us to how information should be validated or invalidated. Besides the job of reading for comprehension is the reading of news information, which means reading not once and not through just one source but through various platforms and modalities. This skill must be built into all the current curriculums. Whether it is science and the discussion of topics or words that are controversial, such as "global warming" or "science-based" and "evidence-based," or math and the discussion of pollster numbers, there needs to be a reallocation to understanding how literacy works within the constraints of the news information (Domonoske 2017). In the role of the school library, there is an opportunity for this discourse to be examined and studied with multiple sources of information. Also, the library exists as a place where everyone's thinking should be welcome and where respectful dialogue can ensue. There has never been a time quite a like this period in our history when we need these places for learning to exist so that students can delve into that type of thinking—and frankly the library is a safe space to grow such concepts and thoughts. The idea of misreading information should be at the forefront of everything we do as information and media literacy leaders, researchers, and educators.

IGNORED

Validate, validate, validate! The ignoring of obvious information is quite clear and very apparent in the way information is projected through news agencies. However, I need to preface this by saying that ignoring is primarily done through the opinion makers and gatherers, which is where most of the 24-hour news cycle appears to be on any given day. The way news is projected begs the question, "What is being missed because visual cues aren't seen?" This question very much takes me back to the U.S. presidential election of 2016, in which the preponderance of polls incorrectly predicted that Hillary Clinton would win. How could the polls be so wrong? The question "Who was being omitted from the message?" comes to mind very quickly. More importantly, what would we have seen if we were just present in the moment and not ignoring some of the more obvious facts, such as the number of Trump signs or the people who were voting one way but who were willing to tell pollsters something different? Why would they offer false information about their voting intentions? The answer: Because they were already discouraged by the members of the media who, they felt, were lacking in their representation of their interests and concerns.

Quite often, our social and group bubbles—family, friends, religious affiliations, and others—have kept us from seeing a perspective from the other side, whatever that side may be, thus creating a culture of ignorance. Spreading false information is not necessarily caused by malicious intent but because people haven't extended their thinking or their presence into other places, other reading material, or other avenues that would provide for the development of a more informed viewpoint. After the election of 2016, this became a very big part of the conversation in many communities, whether local, school, or academic. Emily Bailin Wells, a doctoral candidate at Teachers College of Columbia University blogged about this sentiment right after the election:

> This is our country. This is *our* America. If you are surprised, it means your beliefs—what you want to be good and true in this world—have been disrupted. Your bubble of reality has been pinpricked; perhaps it's burst completely. This morning, a reality outside of your purview, of your wildest imagination, set in. My bubble included. New York City is a bubble that provided me (and so many others) a false sense of security and hope in the last few weeks, especially yesterday. I feel ignorant. Embarrassed. Naive. This country is so much bigger than my little privileged liberal bubble. (Wells, 2016)

Wells was one among many from various political perspectives who, whether due to righteousness, naïveté, or just because of their own political ideology, were not seeing that there existed much more of a divide in our country than we had thought. A few months after the election in a high-profile article, danah boyd argued that media literacy education had backfired, becoming one of the many reasons why there was such a divide—not just politically but educationally and even among the media. As can be imagined, this article caused a stir among media literacy educators. It provided another look at how assumptions can mask what is really going on.

In order for media literacy to have, as boyd states, "backfired," there needed to be a formulated practice of media literacy education in place. Education programs would have had to have some instituted, implemented, or mandated curriculum that was driven and modeled for teachers. This has not occurred for quite some time despite the fact that over 20 years of work has been devoted to bringing media and information literacy to the forefront of education. In most cases, specific teachers in specific subject areas or librarians who teach critical thinking skills are the sole voice for this type of instruction. But those subject areas have been minimized, diminished, or eliminated because they have are perceived to lack value or are not assessed in some way that produces data for assessment purchases. In most schools, literacy instruction is still limited to reading and writing and not considered in the greater context of media in whatever form that it comes today.

The wider assumption in boyd's article was that media literacy education had been happening but had somehow failed. The truth is that media literacy has been struggling to gain recognition and value in education for quite some time—some would even say as far back as the 1960s. In fact, media literacy education proponents are largely voiceless in a stream of policy and research that is data driven but that cares very little for the individual child. Most educators, whether vested in media literacy, in information literacy, or in general education, work with students and know that they have questions about media sources and information credibility—concerning and disturbing questions—but practitioners are not given the time, the opportunity, or the ability to engage with students on that level.

More problematic than when policy and researchers drive change in education is when they are not involved in education at all or when their impact is limited by virtue of their coming in to collect data, prioritizing academic data gathering over action research that could have more immediate benefits for students. That is not to say that there is no value in traditional academic research. Obviously, that would be a false statement, but when research dictates change alone without having those who are on the ground working with students as participants, then we have a bigger problem. This point demonstrates the issue that we face in education where policy has been top-down and not from the grassroots, from educators who work tirelessly with students and families in every aspect of their lives.

Here is another consideration: Large-scale education data mined with automated algorithms lacks a human connection. These types of studies don't look at the thoughts and sentiments of individuals and their experiences. They don't give voice to human emotion, culture, upbringing, or strong beliefs that have been ingrained through time. They don't recognize the voiceless in our society because they don't see them and they aren't participating in a computational equation that has been manufactured by a researcher. Sweeping generalities have been a significant part of the issue when it comes to media consumption, viewing, and creation. Isn't this what the predominant media managed to forget when they were looking at polling data and not seeing the greater population? The fourth estate forgot to do its job by looking at the whole public, the whole nation. They represented themselves and not the people they were supposed to be watching and reporting.

Unfortunately, media and information literacy is also at times driven by a particular ideological agenda instead of providing an unbiased platform for multiple thinking and multiple pedagogical considerations. What is most frustrating in this day and age is that many people have taken on group-think behavior so that dialogue representing multiple perspectives is not well received or wanted. The "need to be right" is more important than the need to "bridge" ideas. Most of us want to be aware and to have a critical voice. Most educators strive for those slim moments when dialogue can lead to enlightenment. Most media and information literacy educators truly have the best interests of their work in front of them. What we need is the opportunity to ignite the fire, which can very well be done in the school library media center.

CULTURE OF INQUIRY

Students need to be encouraged to ask questions in an open culture of inquiry. As organizations that facilitate information access, school libraries provide a natural context for such a culture. For effective media literacy education, an open culture of inquiry should be combined with wide availability of resources and easy access to information. Thus, there is already a synergistic fit between library resources and services and an open culture of inquiry.

As Toffler (1984) states, "The illiterate of the 21st century will not be those who cannot read and write, but those who cannot learn, unlearn, and relearn" (p. 414). We are in need of teaching our students to become a part of the learning cycle in order to grow into the community and future that they will face directly in a global world. This must also be true for our teachers, as the cycle of learning in education must be a continuous and well-defined process. Instituting strands of technological learning incorporated into the curriculum must be perceived as authentic by students and by teachers. Too often, reforms in education appear contrived and forced to both educators and students. As Ken Robinson confirms:

> The fact is that given the challenges we face, education doesn't need to be reformed—it needs to be transformed. The key to this transformation is not to standardize education, but to personalize it, to build achievement on discovering the individual talents of each child, to put students in an environment where they want to learn and where they can naturally discover their true passions. (Robinson 2011, p. 35)

The value of media literacy is that it "promotes critical thinking beyond the traditional literacies of reading and writing, including visual and computer literacies" (Yildiz and De Abreu 2014, p. 186). In doing so, it enables students take more control of their learning and to reflect on the role of media in their lives. It also moves the role of the educator more toward helping students understand the media. Within both classroom and library settings, there is a need for more effective methods for teaching media literacy skills. One of the most significant ways in which educators (including librarians) can teach media literacy is by facilitating student discourse around the media:

> Increasingly students are swamped with information overload, and they are making decisions and selections based upon what they are told by or through the media. As the information is being forced upon them, many of our students are left to think about what they are seeing and hearing without having a chance for some form of discourse. (Yildiz and De Abreu, 2014, pp. 186–187)

In addition to facilitating student discourse, teachers and librarians can help students to apply critical thinking beyond traditional classroom subjects to the broader media environment—film, television, music, social media, and more. As Victor Strasburger indicates in an interview with the Consortium of Media Literacy:

> What we need to teach is much more about critical thinking, much more about how to decipher all this information that's available on the Internet, some of which may be accurate, some of which may not be accurate—how to deal with tweeting, and texting, and downloading, and we're simply not doing that. (As quoted in Jolls 2015)

With so many different media choices available to today's students, from wide-ranging music and video platforms to countless social media environments, most students are:

> open to being freely engaged online and on multiple platforms such as Instagram, Twitter, Facebook, and others. Students can easily place themselves in the media sphere and do so quite readily. Because it is such an important part of their landscape, the importance of being able to deconstruct what they see, hear, buy, or select makes the teaching of media literacy valuable. (Yildiz and De Abreu 2014, p. 188)

Media literacy can help them to become more informed and more critical consumers, users, and creators of these various media.

CONCLUSION

The rise of misinformation and the direct delivery of that misinformation place school libraries in a vital position for assisting students to think critically about media messages. As curators and aggregators of data, school libraries, particularly school library media specialists, have the capacity to provide ample and ongoing meaningful lessons that bring up the level of discourse to engage students to think further on issues presented by the media or in the classroom. Beyond researching for information, the skills that can be developed within this learning space form a continuum for life-long learning.

There is no stopping where the media will take us now or in the future. We can depend on the knowledge that media technology will change and so will the information providers and even the receivers. Therefore, we would be well-advised to consider the role of media and information literacy education as a flexible process for engagement and learning that will be synchronized with the ever growing changes of the media feed.

REFERENCES

Abilock, Debbie. "Information Literacy: From Prehistory to K–20: A New Definition." *Knowledge Quest* 32, no. 4 (2004): 9–11.

American Association of School Librarians. *AASL Standards Framework for Learners*. Chicago: American Library Association, 2018. https://standards.aasl.org/wp-content/uploads/2017/11/AASL-Standards-Framework-for-Learners-pamphlet.pdf.

BBC News. "'Post-Truth' Declared Word of the Year by Oxford Dictionaries." BBC.com, 16 November 2016. http://www.bbc.com/news/uk-37995600.

Domonokse, Camila. "CDC Denies Banning Words; Rights Group Projects Disputed Terms onto Trump D.C. Hotel." NPR, 20 December 2017. https://www.npr.org/sections/thetwo-way/2017/12/20/572242449/as-cdc-denies-banning-words-hrc-projects-disputed-terms-on-trumps-d-c-hotel.

Flood, Alison. "Fake News Is 'Very Real' Word of the Year for 2017." *The Guardian*, 1 November 2017. https://www.theguardian.com/books/2017/nov/02/fake-news-is-very-real-word-of-the-year-for-2017.

Jolls, Tessa. "Voices of Media Literacy: International Pioneers Speak: Victor C. Strasburger, MD." Consortium for Media Literacy, 19 November 2015. http://www.medialit.org/reading-room/voices-media-literacy-international-pioneers-speak-victor-c-strasburger-md.

Roberts, Brian. "The Offensive against the Fourth Estate." *Time & Tide: The Independent Weekly*, 36 (29 October 1955): 1395.

Robinson, Ken. *Out of Our Minds: Learning to Be Creative*. Chichester: Capstone Publishing, 2011.

Thoman, Elizabeth, and Tessa Jolls. *Literacy for the 21st Century: An Overview & Orientation Guide to Media Literacy Education*. Malibu, CA: Center for Media Literacy, 2003. http://www.medialit.org/sites/default/files/01_MLKorientation.pdf.

Toffler, Alvin. *Future Shock*. New York: Bantam Books, 1984.

Wells, Emily B. ". . . Now What?" My [Media]ted Life, 9 November 2016. https://mymediatedlifeblog.com/2016/11/09/now-what/.

Yildiz, Melda N., and Belinha De Abreu. "Fostering Global Literacies among Pre-Service Teachers through Innovative Transdisciplinary Projects." In Jared Keengwe, Grace Onchwari, and Darrell Hucks (eds.), *Literacy Enrichment and Technology Integration in Pre-Service Teacher Education*, 183–201. Hershey, PA: IGI Global, 2014.

ELEVEN

Cultivating Students as Educated Citizens: The Role of Academic Libraries

Hailey Mooney, Jo Angela Oehrli, and Shevon Desai

> The silver lining to the dark cloud of fake news is that academic librarians have a whole host of examples and connections to draw upon that can wake students up to the very visceral and real impacts of information production and consumption.

In the fall of 2016, "fake news" began to dominate news headlines and fuel public discourse. Libraries have a long history of working to strengthen the information literacy skills of our patrons, and one can easily view the fake news phenomenon as just the most recent iteration. Rather than cynically accept the current state of affairs as inevitable, at the University of Michigan (U-M) Library, we wanted to take advantage of this unique cultural moment to emphasize the importance of information literacy now more than ever. We had the opportunity to create a one-credit course focusing on fake news and in doing so came to recognize that this was the perfect opportunity to engage both students and our broader community in a much larger discussion about critical thinking in the current information environment.

Fake news has been used as a catchall phrase that means different things to different people. The bigger landscape of misinformation and disinformation reveals a nuanced, complicated issue that reveals the importance of critical thinking and evaluation skills. As librarians, we struggled to address this complicated landscape in a meaningful way, realizing that taking a simple checklist approach (e.g., "five easy things you can do to fight fake news!") would be doing a disservice to our community. As much as we could, we strived to provide resources (instruction, guides, community events, workshops, and more) that did not dumb down what is a complex problem.

In terms of instruction, what fake news has made painfully evident is that our goals for the classroom must extend beyond merely equipping students to complete the immediate assignment at hand. Every instruction session is an opportunity to impart the lifelong learning goals that are embedded in the Association of College & Research Libraries' (ACRL) *Framework for Information Literacy for Higher Education.* Indeed, it is inspiring to remind ourselves that one of the larger goals of liberal arts–centered higher education is to create citizens who embody moral and social responsibility (Association of American Colleges & Universities 2007). An approach to instruction that considers these big-picture goals is critical pedagogy, which endeavors to integrate social justice aims, such as to support a democratic society wherein informed citizens actively participate in their own governance and are capable of gaining legitimate knowledge about their communities.

In our case, it became clear that the community itself also has a strong desire for a deeper understanding of the fake news problem within the larger information environment and for stronger information literacy skills to deal with the increasingly complicated demands on us as information consumers. The enormous public response to a single press release announcing the library's development of a course focusing on fake news (Piñon 2017) took us by surprise. Within a few short months, we had done dozens of news interviews with numerous local, national, and international media outlets, participated on a local YV news talk show, were invited to join journalist panel discussions, been asked to participate in many local and national events, and were regularly fielding questions about the course itself.

In considering all the activities and resources related to fake news that we have undertaken, the following chapter addresses in more detail those that are transferrable to other libraries and the most relevant to developing critical thinking skills within the context of the current information landscape of misinformation and disinformation. We discuss the range of engagement that librarians at U-M have had with fake news, from the development of the fake news course itself, with the associated media and community outreach opportunities, to how fake news has impacted our approach to traditional one-shot instruction sessions. Informing all of our fake news efforts has been a philosophy of encouraging deeper engagement with the issues affecting our information environment.

U-M LIBRARY'S ENGAGEMENT WITH FAKE NEWS

During the development of the fake news course, as well as the creation of research guides and one-shot instruction sessions, and throughout our interactions with the media and community organizations, our emphasis has been on critical thinking as a higher-order thinking skill. At the same time, we recognize that this is not something that can be learned in an hour but is rather the beginning of a discussion—a gateway to developing lifelong skills as a critical consumer of information.

The Class

In the winter 2017 semester, Doreen Bradley, U-M Library's director of learning programs and initiatives, had a casual conversation with an assistant dean at the College of Literature, Science, and the Arts (LSA) about offering a minicourse focused on fake news. Doreen brought in Shevon Desai, communication studies librarian, Hailey Mooney, psychology & sociology librarian, and Angie Oehrli, a learning librarian. The team put together a course proposal that was quickly accepted by LSA and spent the summer of 2017 developing course content. The minicourse was to be a one-credit, undergraduate class that met for seven weeks. Angie would be the instructor. While there were several learning outcomes for the class, the larger, critical thinking outcomes included that students would be able to:

- critically evaluate news sources in order to determine content credibility;
- analyze the impact of psychological and social factors on media consumption in order to reflect on their own personal media consumption behaviors and practices; and
- discuss the individual and societal impacts of news literacy in order to understand its importance to public policy and democracy.

The focus of the course materials was to emphasize critical thinking about the news. We were interested in creating exercises that helped students develop and implement a personal strategy to make an informed opinion about current topics so that they could become better informed citizens. For example, many infographics have been created to help news readers develop a checklist whenever they engage with the news. Instead of proposing one of the many infographics as a recommended framework for identifying fake news, we gathered multiple infographics together and asked students to compare the strategies proposed in them. The students applied the infographic strategies to several news articles and then determined the strengths and weaknesses of each set of strategies.

Other critical thinking activities included exercises examining journalism ethics, interpreting data visualizations, and debating the value of the 24-hour news cycle. In many cases, exercises from the class could be used in the library's engagement with fake news in other venues, such as informal teaching opportunities, media interviews, or community talks. A description of the numerous ways our library has brought components of the for-credit fake news class to engage in outreach and community discussion is provided later in this chapter. In other more traditional cases, like course-integrated instruction sessions, core concepts and the ethos of critical thinking can be integrated.

EXTENDING CRITICAL THINKING ABOUT FAKE NEWS INTO TRADITIONAL CLASSROOM INSTRUCTION

Regardless of what it's called, fake news as a social phenomenon has been and will continue to be a part of the information landscape regardless of whether or not it garners the necessary interest in your community to merit press attention, community event invitations, and the opportunity to teach a dedicated course. An important outcome of the development of the fake news class was the opportunity to reflect on the overall impacts of current events and the disordered state of the information environment on our everyday classroom instruction. Fake news offers a cultural touchpoint that can be extended to make scholarly information seeking and evaluation more relatable. This section details how the overall philosophy of our fake news instruction, based on a critical pedagogy of developing higher-order thinking skills and reflective practice, can be extended to traditional classroom instruction based on teaching the scholarly literature review.

Regardless of the specific class and assignment, the crux of most academic library instruction revolves around finding and evaluating sources. To contextualize these essential information literacy concepts and skills within a society with a fake news problem is to engage with critical pedagogy and to see information literacy as a contested part of an overall education system and information environment that reflects oppressive power structures (Tewell 2015). The ability of some information to be made more visible and spread across social networks, as we have seen with the spread of fake news, demonstrates this problematic structure and the manipulation by powerful actors that occurs in the current state of "information disorder" (Wardle and Derakhshan 2017) in which students must function. Even a course-related assignment that limits students to using scholarly journal articles still requires engagement and contextualization within the broader information environment. That is to say, all information literacy opportunities are critical information literacy opportunities, and fake news has impacted the information environment in ways that cannot be ignored.

As an additional foundation to this approach, consider that scholarly research doesn't happen in a vacuum. In fact, the whole point of scholarship is to provide a feedback loop to improve our everyday world. Ideally, the policies that shape civil society have some basis in evidence. A key issue of fake news is the obfuscation of evidence in favor of information that supports policies serving limited interests for selected gains (as opposed to societal interests for the greater good). To the extent that scholarly research is evidence, it is also subject to being faked or taken out of context in order to serve the purposes of fakery. This has been true for hundreds of years, even before Thomas Carlyle bemoaned that "a witty statesman might prove anything by statistics" (1840, p. 9), to the myriad examples we have of today's fake news.

Making Critical Connections

With a little creativity and forethought, it is possible to take any component of an instruction session and draw out a relationship to the real world, fake news, and critical thinking. In other words, you can "hide carrots in their brownies" and incorporate critical information literacy into any class (Seale 2016). On the flip side, the silver lining to the dark cloud of fake news is that academic librarians have a whole host of examples and connections to draw upon that can wake students up to the very visceral and real impacts of information production and consumption.

Here is an approach to making critical connections happen:

1. *Call it out.* Question the reasoning behind the assignment requirements or recommended information practice in order to draw out the larger purpose and big-picture lifelong learning goals.

2. *Contextualize.* Situate concepts and skills in the broader information environment, both:

    a. within scholarly communication and disciplinary practices, and

    b. outward to current events and societal issues.

3. *Connect.* Bring it back to the assignment at hand in order to promote critical engagement with the required task.

Note that, despite the numbered list, this is not a definitive checklist for bringing critical thinking into the library classroom. Remember, our approach to addressing fake news is to move beyond the checklist. This is a starting point for engaging with any typical literature review assignment in a way that makes explicit connections to the liberal arts learning goal to create informed citizens who can apply classroom learning to the real world.

Examples

Let's look at some examples that show how connections to fake news can be drawn when teaching to the common assignment to write a topic paper supported by gathering a small set of scholarly journal articles, for example, find three peer-reviewed articles about your topic.

Assignment Requirement to Find Multiple Sources

1. Call it out.

Ask students: "Why would reliance on a single source be insufficient to understand a topic?" An assignment based on finding more than one source poses an opportunity to discuss the verification process as a search and evaluation strategy. A verification process of consulting multiple sources is needed in order to understand the full range of knowledge on a particular topic and determine consensus.

2. Contextualize.

In fact, the literature review section of an empirical journal article is an exercise in this very process, detailing the previous research that undergirds and pertains to the study at hand. Here is a chance to connect to current events in academia: the rise of the systematic review. Traditionally a technique in evidence-based medical and health sciences research, systematic reviews are being increasingly called for in the social sciences. The idea is that a systematic and transparent approach to literature reviews (not necessarily a full-fledged systematic review using protocols and published as a stand-alone paper) will reduce bias and cherry-picking of sources that support the author's preferred viewpoint (e.g., Albarracín 2015).

Next, build a bridge back to the real world. What sort of bias and cherry-picking of sources occur there? Does your Facebook news feed present a straightforward view of the world? Is there some recent event in the news or policy making that might showcase overreliance on some sources or viewpoints? For example, a tax plan that significantly reduces the corporate tax rate is likely based on the theory of trickle-down economics. Have you heard any news reports that present a balanced literature review on the veracity of trickle-down economics?

3. Connect.

Finally, bring it back to the assignment. What considerations should students make when choosing sources for their bibliographies? They can make their points stronger by citing multiple sources that show the same thing or even by seeking out systematic reviews and using them as a valuable and high-impact source type. They should seek to carefully choose a well curated and representative sample of articles showcasing the range of research findings on a given topic. Not just the first three somewhat relevant articles that come up in their search results.

Assignment Requirement to Find Peer-Reviewed Articles

1. Call it out.

Another part of helping students complete that common peer-reviewed article assignment is a discussion of peer review itself. Ask the students: "Why are scholarly articles peer reviewed?" How does the process help to ensure the integrity of the information? Different publication processes differentiate types of sources and can serve as shorthand for determining credibility.

2. Contextualize.

Most academic librarians can give an explanation, in their sleep, of the purpose of peer review and how it works. We might end by saying that the system is imperfect and has some associated debates as to how peer review should be accomplished. But here is another opportunity to go a little deeper.

Peer review can be and is sometimes faked. So-called predatory journals are an example. Unsuspecting (or complicit) scholars submit their publications to journals that claim to provide quick turnaround times to publication and open access to articles in exchange for an Article Processing Charge (Cress 2017). Another way to fake peer review is for a seemingly legitimate publication to act as a mouthpiece for corporate and industry interests. Editorial boards and authors can have academic credentials but may be acting in the interests of hidden entities that fund their work. For example, consider the publication of scientific research that is used to support industrial practices and consumer products that overall scientific consensus finds to be harmful (Zou 2016). Tread carefully; don't sow too much additional skepticism because students need to develop trust in science in a world of postmodern constructed truths (Barclay 2017), but do introduce some shades of gray.

3. Connect.

Despite some discussion of the reliability of peer review, the peer reviewed article is the gold standard for publishing scholarly research, and this is why literature review assignments typically contain requirements for including peer reviewed journal articles. Taking the extra step to verify the authenticity of a publication, including the authority of authors and editors, may sometimes be necessary to confirm trustworthiness.

Assignment Requirement (or Recommendation) to Use a Library Database

1. Call it out.

Students will need to be directed to an appropriate database for locating scholarly articles to complete their assignment. So let's look at tools for locating information. What is the current dominant cultural paradigm for finding information? "Just Google it, stupid." Moving students away from Google and toward library databases is usually part of any information literacy session. How much time do you devote to really explaining why Google is problematic? Why is overreliance on any one tool problematic? Choosing a search tool is an opportunity to exercise critical thinking. There are actually many more options than to "just Google it." Making students aware of these options is one thing; helping them to practice evaluation of search *resources* (in addition to sources) is another.

2. Contextualize.

Here's what we learned from fake news and its attendant issues: The technologies that we use to find out about the world are not neutral, and they do not always surface the "right" answer to the very top. Databases and search engines have producers with motives and objectives. Decisions are made on what to include and exclude. Algorithms are constructed by people who have made value judgments as to what is relevant or not. Databases and search engines have varying levels of transparency or opaqueness regarding how they work and what sources they include. Search engines are not oracles; they are reflections of our society. In a society where fake news and other forms of information obfuscation are commonplace, it is important to be aware that the tools we use to find information are also susceptible to manipulation. An entire sector of the marketing industry is devoted to search engine optimization, and propagandists employ their own set of methods to inflate the rankings of conspiracy theorists and other sources of fake news that further their aims.

Most library databases also have proprietary relevancy-ranking algorithms that are not disclosed, but other aspects of their content and functioning are more transparent. Journal coverage lists detail exactly which titles are included. Multiple sort functions are available so that one need not rely exclusively on the algorithmic relevancy rank. This puts more control in the hands of the researcher to dictate the search and display of the results. Importantly, library databases do not make their profits from the business model of surveillance capitalism. Libraries and the researchers they represent are the direct customers, not advertisers representing business and political interests.

3. Connect.

An introduction to the recommended library databases for the class that elucidates these broader points will provide an entry by which to highlight the advanced features of the database and provide students with some evaluative criteria for what to look for when using a variety of different search tools. Instead of telling students to use PsycINFO or whatever database because it's simply what you recommend, explain why and provide reflection points regarding the differences between that database and the familiar Google search engine.

Practical Considerations

Make sure that the big picture and current event examples stay within the parameters of the class and assignment. Subject specialist librarians have the advantage of familiarity with the specific scholarly communication practices of the discipline and disciplinary outlooks. Bringing to light tacit disciplinary practices in knowledge creation and dissemination furthers critical information literacy aims (Simmons 2005), and understanding disciplinary approaches to the construction of knowledge can inform understanding of popular ways of knowing. What is the lens that the subject matter of the course provides, and how can you leverage it to deepen your instruction of information literacy concepts? For example, a sociological or feminist approach to information systems reveals the way that search engine algorithms reflect gender and racial bias. A psychology class might discuss cognitive biases that obscure the rational evaluation of information. Find the intersections, and bring them to light.

Talk with the course instructor, and make sure that your learning goals are aligned. Streamline the number of learning goals you plan to cover in your session in order to allow time for bringing to light big-picture connections and for including higher-order thinking skills. (In any case, limiting learning goals generally makes one-shot sessions more manageable.) If you want to plan on some extra discussion time to make explicit connections to fake news in a class focused on scholarly journal articles, then practice the discussion with the instructor first. When you meet with the instructor to discuss the class lesson plan, bring up the critical connections that you see between the assignment and real-world information seeking. This can be part of the natural lesson planning discussion. Instructors may not have considered a critical information literacy angle before and are often receptive to integrating these ideas into the class.

Other Library Engagement

Outside the classroom and curriculum, many in the general public are also deeply interested in understanding the fake news issue and promoting the value of critical thinking. The media attention that our for-credit fake news class received led to intense community interest, including invitations to engage in multiple fake news activities both within and outside the university community. While some of the activities were curriculum based, others had a more external component. We found that it was important to talk about the complexity of fake news at events outside the university. In reminding people that libraries are key places where the general population can engage in discourse about important topics, team members have been able to "show up" in the public debate about fake news. The theme of critically thinking about the news has consistently emerged.

Informal Teaching Opportunities

We created a research guide on fake news (http://guides.lib.umich.edu/fakenews) that has an instructional focus. With sections such as "How Do You Recognize Bias in Yourself and in the Media?" and "Why Is [Fake News] Important?" we wanted to focus more on the questions that can be asked by anyone who is reading news of any kind and not just recommend one strategy or type of Web site. There is a page on the research guide explaining where specific media outlets fall on the political spectrum. This spectrum is not a binary analysis of media sources but instead describes multiple types of political thought, as well as giving an understanding of how those perspectives were identified. This research guide gives the readers multiple approaches for dealing with fake news and does not espouse a checklist approach to the news, instead presenting a more nuanced approach to understanding issues of source evaluation and credibility.

Other teaching opportunities have included partnering in both a Teach Out and a Teach In about fake news. The Teach Out was coordinated by U-M's Office of Academic Innovation and was a digital education opportunity freely open to members of the public. The Teach In was directed by the History Department and was a three-hour session in which the history of fake news was discussed, and we engaged the audience in critical discussions in both small-group and large-group settings. Questions we asked during the Teach In included, "What is fake news?" and "How can you help stop the spread of fake news?" Again, these questions focused more on the complex issues of fake news rather than on simplifying the fake news problem by proposing one solution. The librarians who codeveloped the course have been asked to do one-shot library workshops, as well as to be guest lecturers for U-M classes, and they have even considered developing a digital learning object to help students engage with the news in general.

Noncurricular Teaching Opportunities

Other educational opportunities have been less curriculum based and can be divided into three categories: campus engagement, library community interest, and community/general public engagement. On campus, we have participated in a residence hall event, a graduate student case competition centered on fake news, and consulted with a student organization. The Learning Librarian, who was the instructor for the class, will participate as a guest speaker for two different campus conferences: the U-M Women of Color Task Force Annual Conference and a student-led conference at the U-M School of Information. Our goal for accepting these invitations is not to lecture the audience about fake news. Rather, we want to provide critical thinking opportunities that we can work through with the attendees.

One of the most interesting campus engagement opportunities involved working with an undergraduate student to create a series of educational slides featured on the Undergraduate Library's digital screen array. Much like the librarians, this student wanted to convey the complexity of the issue by avoiding the checklist approach to fake news. The Learning Librarian met with the student several times to develop a series of questions that would help students engage with news in general. As an art student, the student then developed an artistic theme in a slide show that centered on the spreading of a fire to help in conveying critical thinking questions visually. These slides have been featured multiple times in the library.

Within the library community, two U-M librarians participated in the June 2017 Library Journal webinar series entitled "Fighting Fake News," in which they described some of U-M's efforts in addressing fake news, as well as offering other educational ideas. Critical thinking was also emphasized in that setting. For example, we suggested asking students for their own personal definitions of fake news before offering any of the standard definitions so that they could apply their own experiences of engaging with the news before seeing how someone else defined it. One of us has participated in a conversation with Alison J. Head, the principal investigator of the ACRL cofunded project, How Do Students Consume News?—a conversation that included other librarians who are addressing the issue of fake news. The instructor for the class has also presented at the fall 2017 Association of Research Libraries meeting to inform ARL library directors of different ways that libraries can "tackle" fake news. She has also completed interviews with library organizations, including the Michigan Academic Library Association. The U-M team has shared instruction ideas with other libraries. In sharing U-M's ideas with the larger library community on how to critically engage with fake news, it is hoped that educational opportunities will arise where thoughtful approaches can be applied to encountering the news rather than using a checklist method.

The U-M Library has been approached by several groups in the Ann Arbor area and across the state of Michigan to talk about fake news. These groups include a local church, a Kiwanis Club, an interview for a student project at another local college, and a speaking engagement at a community college on the other side of the state. At this time, most of these engagements have not yet been completed, but we're planning that, instead of a lecture-based lesson on one strategy of how to encounter the news, the speakers at these events will work to create critical thinking environments via discussions and interactive exercises.

The last significant area where U-M has engaged with the issue of fake news has been with the media. The media itself is a huge stakeholder in the issues surrounding fake news. In our conversations with the media, we have tried to emphasize the complex nature of the dissemination of fake news and how misleading information can be confusing. We want the public to know that the library is an important place where difficult issues can be explored. The university put forward a press release when the course was approved, and the Associated Press picked up the story. We have been interviewed by local and Detroit media outlets and have served on a Sunday morning panel show, on a statewide public radio, and in multiple college newspapers. One of us was interviewed by *Vice Magazine*, which garnered a lot of attention. Internationally, we have been interviewed by reporters in Canada, Ireland, Germany, and Sweden. We were even invited to participate in a Detroit Press Club panel event.

CONCLUSION

At the U-M Library, we had the unique opportunity to develop and teach a stand-alone course devoted to fake news. The course has served as fertile soil for the cultivation multiple of information literacy efforts focused on growing educated and critically minded citizens. Even if you can't devote an entire class to fake news, a few editorial comments that bring assignments into a critical social context and making time for some brief related discussions can go a long way toward integrating real-world learning into what would otherwise be a rote instruction session. As students, our favorite teachers were always those who took "bird walks"—bringing in personal stories or discussing current events and artfully tying them back to the course content. These real-world connections make classes interesting and keep students engaged.

Grappling with the issues attendant to fake news can sometimes feel controversial and difficult. Critical engagement with the disordered information environment can involve calling out problematic social issues and making evident the role of powerful actors that aren't always in the best interests of civic society. It is our professional duty as academic librarians to help students develop the knowledge and skills needed to critically engage in information seeking and evaluation, both within the academy and outside the university. Bringing attention to challenges in the information environment is not the same as promoting a particular ideological viewpoint; we want students to think for themselves and move beyond uncritically endorsing information simply because it supports their preexisting beliefs.

The media exposure and community-wide attention that our fake news minicourse received has been edifying in affirming the desire of most people to be informed and to participate in a functional democratic society

fueled by real news. It has strengthened our commitment to critical information literacy and to cultivating students as educated citizens.

REFERENCES

Albarracín, Dolores. "Editorial." *Psychological Bulletin* 141, no. 1 (2015):
    1–5. https://doi.org/10.1037/bul0000007
Association of American Colleges & Universities and National Leadership
    Council (U.S.). *College Learning for the New Global Century: A
    Report from the National Leadership Council for Liberal Educa-
    tion & America's Promise*. Washington, DC: Association of Amer-
    ican Colleges, 2007.
Barclay, D. A. "The Challenge Facing Libraries in an Era of Fake News."
    The Conversation, 4 January 2017. http://theconversation.com/the
    -challenge-facing-libraries-in-an-era-of-fake-news-70828.
Carlyle, Thomas. *Chartism*. London: J. Fraser, 1840.
Cress, Phaedra. "Guest Post: When Authors Get Caught in the Predatory
    (Illegitimate Publishing) Net." *The Scholarly Kitchen*, 11 Decem-
    ber 2017. https://scholarlykitchen.sspnet.org/2017/12/11/guest-post
    -authors-get-caught-predatory-illegitimate-publishing-net/.
Piñon, A. "Library Battles Fake News with New Class." *Michigan News,*
    17 February 2017. https://www.lib.umich.edu/news/library-battles
    -fake-news-new-class.
Seale, Maura. (2016). "Carrots in the Brownies: Incorporating Critical
    Librarianship in Unlikely Places." In Nicole Pagowsky and Kelly
    McElroy (eds.), *Critical Library Pedagogy Handbook*, Volume 1,
    pp. 229–232). Chicago: Association of College and Research
    Libraries. http://mauraseale.org/wp-content/uploads/2016/03/mseale
    -carrots-in-brownies.pdf.
Simmons, Michelle Holschuh. "Librarians as Disciplinary Discourse Medi-
    ators: Using Genre Theory to Move toward Critical Information
    Literacy." *portal: Libraries and the Academy* 5, no. 3 (2005): 297–311.
    https://doi.org/10.1353/pla.2005.0041.
Tewell, Eamon. "A Decade of Critical Information Literacy: A Review of
    the Literature." *Communications in Information Literacy* 9, no. 1
    (2015): 24–43. http://www.comminfolit.org/index.php?journal=cil&
    page=article&op=view&path%5B%5D=v9i1p24.

Wardle, Claire, and Hossein Derakhshan. *Information Disorder: Toward an Interdisciplinary Framework for Research and Policy Making.* Strasbourg: Council of Europe, 2017. https://rm.coe.int/information -disorder-report-november-2017/1680764666.

Zou, Jie Jenny. "Brokers of Junk Science?" The Center for Public Integrity, 18 February 2016. https://www.publicintegrity.org/2016/02/18 /19307/brokers-junk-science.

TWELVE

"Survey Says . . .": Developing Students' Critical Data Literacy

Caitlin Shanley and Kristina M. De Voe

> Critical data literacy is an active process that requires engagement
> from data reading to data production.

We are awash in data that we collect, as well as data that is collected about
us, whether it is from alerts on social media, wearable devices that monitor
our individual activities, or persuasive visualizations appearing in news
media or even scientific literature. Contemporary society repeatedly extols
the virtues of big data for revolutionizing our daily lives, in addition to business, medicine, and government, by its ability to discern truth and impact
the future. Yet, in an era of increasing misinformation and disinformation—
one in which *Oxford English Dictionary*'s unironic picks for word of the
year in 2016 and 2017 were "post-truth" (an environment in which people's
beliefs are determined more by personal opinions and emotional appeals
than verifiable facts) and "youthquake" (cultural, political, or social change
instigated by young people), respectively—students assign inordinate levels of authority and objectivity to data, believing that if a number is connected to information, it must be fact (Fontichiaro and Oehrli 2016).

Quantitative evidence, though, can be manipulated, misleading, biased,
or even incomplete across various stages of the overarching data life cycle—
from creation and collection to organization, interpretation, and presentation. Students in colleges and universities need a scaffolded, threshold-based
approach to critical data literacy across the disciplines—from social

sciences to STEM and to even the humanities—in order to become not only better consumers of data but also data creators, enhancing what Wineburg, McGrew, Breakstone, and Ortega (2016) contend is students' "civic online reasoning" (p. 3). With its emphasis on threshold concepts and flexibility, the ACRL *Framework for Information Literacy in Higher Education* (http://acrl.ala.org/framework) provides academic librarians a jumping off point to initiate and extend interdisciplinary conversations with faculty and students about their social responsibilities as readers, communicators, and creators of quantitative evidence.

FROM DATA LITERACY TO CRITICAL DATA LITERACY

The ability to discern quantitative evidence (e.g. raw numbers, graphs, charts, tables, etc.) as information and to derive meaning from it has many names across fields and disciplines. Some call it numeracy, while others use the terms "quantitative reasoning," "quantitative literacy," "statistical literacy," or, more commonly now, "data literacy." For Schield (2004), statistical literacy is the ability to think critically about the use of descriptive statistics (e.g., percentages, averages, and rates) as evidence in arguments, analyzing how the statistics are defined, selected, and presented in a given context (p. 8). This is a "special skill" students must have in conjunction with being data literate: Students must be able to access, assess, manipulate, summarize, and present data (p. 8). Schield sees data literacy, statistical literacy, and information literacy as intrinsically tied together because they involve fundamentals and interdisciplinary study, making them inherently useful to students in any academic major, in addition to librarians seeking additional opportunities to promote critical thinking.

Peter and Kellam (2013) also view statistical literacy as an element of information literacy, spanning a spectrum of skills ranging from "understanding basic statistical terms . . . to more advanced statistical methods and analyses" (p. 2). Koltay (2015) prefers the more straightforward name "data literacy," arguing that a unified terminology and even identity are necessary in order to "convince our stakeholders" of the importance of education surrounding it (p. 403). He recognizes this set of skills as akin to information literacy as well (in addition to a whole host of other literacies), specifying four abilities: "determining when data is needed, accessing sources appropriate to the information need, critically assessing data and their sources and applying results to learning, decision making or problem solving" (p. 405). Koltay's abilities mimic the language used when discussing information literacy, but he also includes the curation of data as a relevant skill. Viewing data in the context of e-research and the data life cycle, Carlson, Fosmire, Miller, and Sapp Nelson (2011) note that production of data as a skill is often overlooked in what they term "data information literacy" programs (p. 6).

Drawing upon social justice educator Paulo Freire's Literacy Method, Tygel and Kirsch (2016) acknowledge the lack of a widely accepted definition of "data literacy" but point to its increasing relevance in order for a literate society not only to understand reality but ultimately to transform the world around them (p. 109). Data literacy for Tygel and Kirsch, however, is a more complex process compared to literacy education, requiring technical capacities and technological access not always available to communities. Indeed, they comment that *data illiteracy* can have "subtle disadvantages" to communities, even impacting individual well-being (p. 113). To reduce such disadvantages and to achieve Freire's emancipatory perspective, Tygel and Kirsch claim that critical analysis of data is necessary; one needs to perceive and problematize data from multiple perspectives (p. 114). They thus call for a "critical data literacy," defining the concept as "a set of abilities which allows one to use and produce data in a critical way" (p. 117). Viewing critical data literacy as a pedagogical methodology, Tygel and Kirsch identify the four abilities: data reading, data processing, data communication, and data production (pp. 117–118). Progressively combined, these can contribute toward transformative action.

CONNECTIONS TO CRITICAL LIBRARIANSHIP AND CRITICAL INFORMATION LITERACY

Building on social justice educators like Freire, librarians have sought to incorporate critical literacy into their practice. The Critlib community, which defines itself as "a movement of library workers dedicated to bringing social justice principles into our work in libraries," has hosted over 100 Twitter chats and several (un)conferences on critical librarianship (Critlib n.d.). The *Journal of Critical Library and Information Studies* published its first two issues in 2017. Librarians continued to explore critical practice with respect to library instruction, as evidenced in books like the 2010 volume *Critical Library Instruction: Theories and Methods* and the 2016 two-volume set *Critical Library Pedagogy*. In a 2006 article on critical information literacy, Elmborg explores the roles of libraries and library educators in cultivating Freirean critical literacy, suggesting that teaching students to adopt a critical consciousness with respect to information is a logical alignment of library values and practice. In Elmborg's vision of critical information literacy, beyond merely learning to use library resources, "students learn to take control of their lives and their own learning to become active agents, asking and answering questions that matter to them and to the world around them" (p. 193).

In 2012, Elmborg reflected on his earlier work and addressed some of the issues that arise in seeking a simple definition of critical information literacy, emphasizing that critical practice "exists in relationships between people and information rather than as an identifiable thing in its own right" (p. 77). Elmborg also calls for a rethinking of the position of the student in information literacy, shifting from the "object" of information literacy to an active participant. Jacobs (2008) emphasizes the role of the librarian in critical information literacy, suggesting that reflective teaching provides a pathway for incorporating critical praxis into library work. She also discusses the difficulty of assessing critical information literacy:

> As a form of literacy, information literacy also operates within a sociopolitical context and is thus politically charged. When we limit its potentials to outcomes and standards, we run the risk of minimizing the complex situated-ness of information literacy and diminishing— if not negating—its inherent political nature. (p. 258)

CONNECTIONS TO THE ACRL FRAMEWORK

When ACRL published the *Information Literacy Competency Standards for Higher Education* in 2000, one of the primary goals was to create a shared set of outcomes that could be used to assess student learning of information literacy competencies. The newer *Framework for Information Literacy for Higher Education* (ACRL 2015) offers a more complex conceptual approach than the older skills-based standards approach, situating information literacy within a multifaceted information ecosystem.[1] Among the necessary areas for development, the authors included, "Students have a greater role and responsibility in creating new knowledge, in understanding the contours and the changing dynamics of the world of information, and in using information, data, and scholarship ethically" (p. 7). This acknowledgment of students as both consumers and creators of information (and data) echoes Elmborg and Jacobs' call to action to rethink the role of the learner in information literacy instruction.

The *Framework* definition of information literacy has four core components: reflective discovery, understanding of production, use in creating new knowledge, and ethical participation. These components reflect the same abilities Tygel and Kirsch lay out in their pedagogical methodology for critical data literacy. Students need to know where and how to find data, and they must know how to troubleshoot when they aren't finding what they need. They must investigate and deduce how data was collected and analyzed. They must use data in their own work as evidence to support their claims. They must use data responsibly and with appropriate credit and attribution. While the *Framework* intends these abilities to apply to many domains, it lays a strong foundation for incorporating industry standard for information literacy into data instruction.

The *Framework* lays out six frames that represent threshold concepts, "frames" meaning, "those ideas in any discipline that are passageways or portals to enlarged understanding or ways of thinking and practicing within that discipline" (p. 7). The six frames (also discussed in Chapter 1 of this volume) focus on (1) the influence of context on authority; (2) the information creation process; (3) the inherent value of information; (4) the connection between research and inquiry; (5) the idea of scholarship as discourse; and (6) the view of information searching as a process of exploration (ACRL 2015).

Each concept is defined and then further explored through knowledge practices and dispositions. The authors describe not just how information literate learners act but also their values and attitudes. While a number of these frames are potentially relevant, we highlight two that have particular relevance for designing library instruction around critical data literacy.

Information Creation as a Process

The Information Creation as a Process frame provides a foundation for thinking of learners as active participants in the data life cycle. This frame posits that format is not the only consideration when selecting a resource; that is, data is not necessarily sufficient to support an argument without careful consideration of how it was created. Students may exhibit tendencies to put greater faith in numbers and statistics, approaching them with less scrutiny than they would other elements of a text. Fontichiaro and Oehrli (2016) write, "Students often believe that numbers are objective, though data in the real world is rarely so. In fact, visualized data—even from authoritative sources—can sometimes be anything but" (p. 22). Furthermore, this frame examines the choices that learners make in their own creation processes, emphasizing the need to consider the impact and message communicated by their chosen format.

When designing learning experiences using this frame, librarians may want to consider the following knowledge practices:

- recognize that information may be perceived differently based on the format in which it is packaged;
- monitor the value that is placed upon different types of information products in varying contexts;
- develop, in their own creation processes, an understanding that their choices impact the purposes for which the information product will be used and the message it conveys. (p. 14)

Information Has Value

Information Has Value describes how information can be considered a commodity and as a way to influence others, in addition to facilitating education and understanding. Beyond just needing specialized skills for searching, learners should understand that access to data in and of itself is political and that even numerical information is not neutral. As the *Framework* puts it, "value may be wielded by powerful interests in ways that marginalize certain voices" (p. 16).

Maksin (2016) explores similar concepts in an article about government information, laying out four core ideas to make government information relevant to students and provide opportunities for critical pedagogy:

- that government information is political,
- that access to government information is political,
- that government information has value both in scholarly contexts and in individuals' daily lives, and
- that we can intervene in the production and dissemination of government information. (p. 122)

Maksin connects the two frames discussed here, emphasizing the role of learners and also the creation and distribution of information. While not all government information is data, these core ideas can be applied to critical data literacy, which also seeks to connect learners' lived experiences to information sources.

Last, the Information Has Value frame calls upon learners to examine power dynamics at play in the information they access, which could have ramifications for how data is collected or represented. When designing learning experiences using this frame, librarians may want to consider the following knowledge practices and dispositions:

- understand how and why some individuals or groups of individuals may be underrepresented or systematically marginalized within the systems that produce and disseminate information;

- recognize issues of access or lack of access to information sources;

- are inclined to examine their own information privilege. (ACRL 2015, p. 6)

In the next section, we will outline strategies for incorporating critical data literacy into library instruction, using tools and techniques borrowed from journalism education.

FACT-CHECKING AND CULTIVATING STUDENTS' CRITICAL DATA LITERACY

Faced with increasing misinformation and disinformation in our radically shifted media ecosystem, journalism educators and journalists have witnessed the growing influence of the fact-checker, as well as a renewed interest in fact-checking as a profession and the fact-checking movement in general (Graves 2016). News outlets have long had their own fact-checking teams, but there has been an infusion of stand-alone fact-checking Web sites and projects, including Snopes, Politifact, and FactCheck.org. Moreover, fact-checking has adapted from merely getting names and dates correct to investigating public figures and critically challenging claims (Canby 2012; Graves 2016). Science journalist and experienced fact-checker, Brooke Borrel, notes that reporters and writers need to apply the tools of fact-checking to their own work by asking themselves:

- Did this happen the way I think it happened?

- Why do I think so?

- Where did I find each of these facts?

- Are my sources trustworthy?

- How do I know this is true? (Borrel 2016, p. 26)

Journalism educator and journalist G. W. Miller III takes this a step further and argues that with bots and algorithms "invading" our newsfeeds, the onus of fact-checking is now on each of us to "go beyond that meme, that random video, or that single story." Miller offers five strategies:

- Look at the other content presented by that source.
- Do a Google search to see if more traditional news organizations covered the stories with similar information.
- Don't ignore the site's advertising.
- Know the difference between facts and assertions.
- Follow the data. (Miller 2018)

In their study of how professional fact-checkers, established scholars, and students determine the credibility of digital information, Wineburg and McGrew (2017) discovered that fact-checkers engaged in more efficient practices for verifying the accuracy of information. They observed that when presented with Web-based tasks, professional fact-checkers first took stock of their bearings and then *read laterally*, meaning they quickly developed a plan and then departed from the site at hand, moving across many connected sites in an attempt to corroborate information (Wineburg and McGrew 2017). As they moved across sites, the fact-checkers attempted to discern what other authorities said about the site; namely, they went in search of additional primary sources. Students and established scholars, however, *read vertically*, remaining on the site at hand longer and becoming caught up in the site's subjective design, its About and History pages, plus their own cognitive biases. Wineburg and McGrew contend that teaching students to read laterally may be more effective than presenting students evaluative checklists.

When examining data, Borrel (2016) points out that fact-checkers aren't expected to be statisticians, but they need to be critical, keeping three things in mind: the context, the source, and common sense. Table 12.1 offers a few considerations for thinking critically about data presented in news media content.

Considering professional fact-checkers techniques and recalling Tygel and Kirsch's four abilities, we can begin to plot learning outcomes that librarians can scaffold and incorporate into their library instruction. Table 12.2 offers examples for connecting critical data literacy abilities to learning outcomes.

Table 12.1 **Consideration for Critical Thinking about Data in the News**

Context	**Big numbers vs. little numbers**. Is the data presented as raw numbers, percentages, fractions, or percentiles? How is the data discussed in relation to accompanying narrative content? For example, natural frequencies (1 in 100) are often easier for readers to understand than using percentages (1%).
	Average is not necessarily what is "typical." How was this "average" calculated? Keep in mind that mean is adding up all of the values and dividing by the quantity of values, median is the middle value, and mode is the most frequent value.
	Sample size. What is the sample size, and how accurately does the sample represent the population? What were the methods for selecting the sample?
	Comparisons. Is the basis for comparison (e.g., over time, group, and/or geography) appropriate and/or logical?
	Reported health risk. What exactly is the risk, how big is it, and whom does it affect? For example, relative risk compares two different test groups, while absolute risk describes the actual likelihood of a specific event happening.
Source	**Identify the origins of the data.** Who produced the data, and how reliable is the source?
	Identify potential biases or conflicts of interest. Is the author/compiler of the data affiliated with a partisan think tank or advocacy group? Has the author/compiler received funding in relation to the data? Is the data confirming my own beliefs?
	Identify the purpose of the data. Why has the data been produced and why now?
	Identify relevant data streams. Can other sources confirm the data? Are they accessible?

(continued)

Table 12.1   (continued)

Common sense	**Do the numbers add up?** For example, in a pie chart, the individual sections should not add up to more than 100 percent.
	Are the axes labeled appropriately? Graphs should have something on their axes. Pay attention to the vertical (y-axis) and whether it includes consistent intervals, misses numbers, or starts at zero.
	Do headlines suggest that one thing caused another? Keep in mind that correlation does not imply causation.
	Does the visualization (graph, chart, table, infographic, etc.) tell a story that accurately reflects the data, or does it tell a story more closely aligned with what the designer would like me to believe? Keep in mind that visualizations can impact the interpretation and analysis of data. Be mindful of color, font, sizes, and design elements.
	What are my emotional interpretation and attachment? Data is not neutral, and data presented visually or in tandem with narrative content can elicit strong emotions—intentionally or unintentionally. Check in with your emotions.

CRITICAL DATA LITERACY THROUGH SKEPTICISM

The skills of verification and fact-checking comprise a crucial part of critical data literacy. Another crucial component is a fundamental shift in how learners approach information, moving from implicit trust to persistent skepticism. These combined skill sets form what Boczkowski (2017) calls "the kernel of an ongoing revolution in interpretive practices." Boczkowski continues:

> Users are becoming ever more skeptical about the information they encounter in the news and social media. And that's a good thing. Skepticism is a necessary, albeit not sufficient, condition for the emergence of sustainable solutions regarding a potential state of misinformation marking contemporary politics and culture.

Table 12.2   Critical Data Literacy Outcomes and Learning Outcome Examples

Tygel and Kirsch's Abilities	Examples of Learning Outcomes
Data reading	• Learners critically analyze the five W's and one H associated with data: where the data came from, who collected the data, what data may/may not be present, why the data may have been collected, when the data was collected, and how the data was collected. • Learners question the logic and suitability of sampling, measurements, comparisons, and/or correlation and causation surrounding the data. • Learners weigh the potential explicit and implicit bias in the data.
Data processing	• Learners can articulate their need to compile and analyze data. • Learners seek out data in relevant collections, recognizing that some data may not be freely available. • Learners select appropriate tools and/or techniques to aid in data compilation and analysis.
Data communicating	• Learners recognize that data can be presented in various ways (e.g., verbally, written, visually), choosing the most appropriate form and/or visualization (e.g., graph, chart, table, map, infographic, etc.). • Learners identify relevant audience(s) with whom to share data, crafting communication to meet larger rhetorical goals. • Learners use data ethically, avoiding misrepresentation of data and acknowledging data source(s) through appropriate citation.

(continued)

Table 12.2   (continued)

Tygel and Kirsch's Abilities	Examples of Learning Outcomes
Data production	• Learners apply their data reading, processing, and communicating abilities to create new data.
	• Learners provide relevant contextual and/or descriptive information associated with their data for data seekers.
	• Learners make their data available and accessible to the widest possible audience.

Skepticism already appears in journalistic practice. *A Dictionary of Journalism* defines skepticism as, "a questioning approach to statements, evidence, received opinions, common sense, and anything that initially appears to be blindingly obvious. Some journalists refer to their sense of skepticism as a built-in 'bullshit detector'" (Harcup 2016). In addition to having students practice the steps of fact-checking, librarians can prompt students to examine their own habits of mind by invoking skepticism in all discussions of data.

By encouraging students to participate actively in data production, librarians can guide them toward skepticism without venturing too far toward cynicism. Based on research studying postsecondary media literacy, Mihailidis (2009) suggests that teaching students only to critique might encourage them to approach media with distrust and cynicism, which could cause them to withdraw rather than participate. He writes, "media-literate students should *understand* the social influences of media, be *aware* of the democratic necessity of a media system, and feel *empowered* to be active civic participants" (p. 8). Critical data literacy is an active process that requires engagement from data reading to data production.

IMPLICATIONS FOR CURRICULAR PARTNERSHIPS, LIFELONG LEARNING, AND CIVIC ENGAGEMENT

Enhancing library instruction with critical data literacy creates a renewed opportunity to gain buy-in for information literacy across the campus, including that of faculty and university administration. Over the years, many librarians have made inroads toward curricular integration by supporting program outcomes related to information literacy. For librarians who haven't seen information literacy codified in that way at their institutions or for those who hope to achieve deeper integration within the university curriculum, expanding our skills to support critical data literacy can provide avenues. One selling point could be career preparation. In 2017, the National Association of Colleges and Employers surveyed around 200 employers and found that 67.5 percent look for analytical/quantitative skills on candidates' resumes (National Association of Colleges and Employers 2017). Librarians can also reinforce to faculty that civic online reasoning is not just part of education, it is part of citizenship. Librarians should use, as Tygel and Kirsch describe it, "a pedagogical methodology oriented to understand reality so as to transform it" (p. 109). Beyond a set of "library skills," we can describe our work as a pathway to achieve program-level learning outcomes related to critical thinking and civic engagement, emphasizing process learning over skills acquisition.

Outside higher education, critical data literacy prepares learners to better understand their world and empowers them to participate more fully in democracy. These skills are especially relevant in a time of increased fake news and alternative facts, when partisan divides and distrust are growing ever stronger. In October 2017, the Pew Research Center found that the opinion gap between Republicans and Democrats on a number of political issues is now at its largest since 1994 (p. 7). In a March 2017 article titled "Purple America Has All but Disappeared," Wasserman suggested that regionalism in the United States has increased, pointing out that less than 10 percent of the counties in the United States were decided by voting margins of under 10 percent in the 2016 presidential election (Wasserman 2017). The (re)emergence of calls for significant political, social, and cultural change arising from young people, though, demonstrates that change is in the air. Librarians can and should foster students' critical consumption and creation of quantitative evidence. By introducing and helping to integrate critical data literacy across the disciplines, we can promote opportunities for students to consider multiple perspectives, facilitate deeper understanding, and influence stakeholders for change.

NOTE

1. The media ecosystem perspective views all of the media with which a person interacts as part of an interconnected information and communication ecology where ideas and messages are exchanged, often across different platforms or formats (Hanna, Rohm, and Crittenden 2011).

REFERENCES

ACRL. *Framework for Information Literacy for Higher Education*. Chicago: Association of College and Research Libraries, 2015. http://acrl.ala.org/framework.

Boczkowski, Pablo J. "The Rise of Skeptical Reading." *NiemanLab Predictions for Journalism 2018*, 2017. http://www.niemanlab.org/2017/12/the-rise-of-skeptical-reading/.

Borrel, Brooke. *The Chicago Guide to Fact-Checking*. Chicago: Chicago University Press, 2016.

Canby, Peter. "Fact-Checking at *The New Yorker*," In Victor S. Navasky and Evan Cornog (eds.), *The Art of Making Magazines: On Being an Editor and Other Views from the Industry*, 51–57. Chicago: Chicago University Press, 2012.

Carlson, Jacob, Michael Fosmire, C. C. Miller, and Megan Sapp Nelson. "Determining Data Information Literacy Needs: A Study of Students and Research Faculty." Libraries Faculty and Staff Scholarship and Research Paper 23, Purdue University, 2011. http://docs.lib.purdue.edu/lib_fsdocs/23.

Critlib: Critical Librarianship, in Real Life & on the Twitters. "about/join the discussion," n.d. http://critlib.org/about/.

Elmborg, James. "Critical Information Literacy: Implications for Instructional Practice." *The Journal of Academic Librarianship* 32, no. 2 (2006): 192–199. https://doi.org/10.1016/j.acalib.2005.12.004.

Elmborg, James. 2012. "Critical Information Literacy: Definitions and Challenges." In Carroll Wetzel Wilkinson and Courtney Bruch (eds.), *Transforming Information Literacy Programs: Intersecting Frontiers of Self, Library Culture, and Campus Community*, 75–80. Chicago: ACRL Press.

Fontichiaro, Kirstin, and Jo Angela Oehrli. "Why Data Literacy Matters." *Knowledge Quest* 44, no. 5 (2016): 20–27. http://www.ala.org/aasl/pubs/kq/v44no5.

Graves, Lucas. *Deciding What's True: The Rise of Political Fact-Checking in American Journalism*. New York: Columbia University Press, 2016.

Hanna, Richard, Andrew Rohm, and Victoria L. Crittenden. "We're All Connected: The Power of the Social Media Ecosystem." *Business Horizons* 54, no. 3 (2011): 265–273. https://wolfman.one/wp-content/uploads/2013/05/BH_HannaRohmCrittenden2011.pdf.

Harcup, Tony (ed.). 2014. "Scepticism." In *A Dictionary of Journalism*. Oxford: Oxford University Press. http://www.oxfordreference.com.

Jacobs, Heidi L. M. "Information Literacy and Reflective Pedagogical Praxis." *The Journal of Academic Librarianship* 34, no. 3 (2008): 256–262.

Koltay, Tibor. "Data Literacy: In Search of a Name and Identity." *Journal of Documentation* 71, no. 2 (2015): 401–415. https://doi.org/10.1108/JD-02-2014-0026.

Maksin, Melanie. 2016. "Of the People, By the People, For the People: Critical Pedagogy and Government Information." In Nicole Pagowsky and Kelly McElroy (eds.), *Critical Library Pedagogy*, Volume 1, 121–130. Chicago: ACRL Press.

Mihailidis, Paul. 2009. "Beyond Cynicism: Media Education and Civic Learning Outcomes in the University." *International Journal of Media and Learning* 1, no. 3 (2009): 1–13. doi:10.1162/ijlm.2009.00027.

Miller III, G. W. "How to Find 'Real News' When Russian Bots and Algorithms Are Invading Your Newsfeed." *The Philadelphia Inquirer*, February 23, 2018. http://www.philly.com/philly/opinion/commentary/fake-news-russian-bots-algorithms-news-literacy-opinion-20180223.html.

National Association of Colleges and Employers (NACE). 2017. "The Key Attributes Employers Seek on Students' Resumes," last modified November 30, 2017. http://www.naceweb.org/about-us/press/2017/the-key-attributes-employers-seek-on-students-resumes/.

Peter, Katharin, and Lynda Kellam. "Statistics & the Single Girl: Incorporating Statistical Literacy into Information Literacy Instruction." *LOEX Quarterly* 40, no. 1 (2013): 2–3, 10. http://commons.emich.edu/loexquarterly/vol40/iss1/2/.

Pew Research Center. "The Partisan Divide on Political Values Grows Even Wider," 2017. http://assets.pewresearch.org/wp-content/uploads/sites/5/2017/10/05162647/10-05-2017-Political-landscape-release.pdf.

Schield, Milo. "Information Literacy, Statistical Literacy and Data Literacy." *IASSIST Quarterly* 28, no. 3 (2004): 6–11. http://www.iassistdata.org/sites/default/files/iqvol282_3shields.pdf.

Tygel, Alan Freihof, and Rosana Kirsch. "Contributions of Paulo Freire for a Critical Data Literacy: A Popular Education Approach." *Journal of Community Informatics* 12, no. 3 (2016): 108–121. http://ci-journal.net/index.php/ciej/article/view/1296.

Wasserman, David. "Purple America Has All but Disappeared." *FiveThir-tyEight*, 8 March 2017. https://fivethirtyeight.com/features/purple -america-has-all-but-disappeared/.

Wineburg, Sam, Sarah McGrew, Joel Breakstone, and Teresa Ortega. *Evaluating Information: The Cornerstone of Civic Online Reasoning.* Stanford History Education Group, 2015. https://stacks.stanford.edu /file/druid:fv751yt5934/SHEG%20Evaluating%20Information%20 Online.pdf.

Wineburg, Sam, and Sarah McGrew. "Lateral Reading: Reading Less and Learning More When Evaluating Digital Information." Stanford History Education Group Working Paper No. 2017-A1, 9 October 2017. http://dx.doi.org/10.2139/ssrn.3048994.

THIRTEEN

Fake News and Academic Librarians: A Hook for Introducing Undergraduate Students to Information Literacy

Carolina Hernandez

> Early reactions to the spread of fake news after the 2016 U.S. presidential election focused on providing checklists that were useful in addressing general concerns about fake news. . . . As shortcuts for identifying fake news, they can draw in students who may be looking for simple solutions. However, they do not help students develop their source evaluation skills.

Fake news is no longer a novel concept. Google Trends shows frequent searches for the phrase "fake news" more than a year after the 2016 U.S. presidential election, which aroused great interest in the topic (Google Trends 2017). After many of the mass shooter incidents in 2017 and 2018, additional waves of fake news spread misinformation about these events (Ansari and Lytvynenko 2017). However, the continuing focus on fake news has obscured the fact that there is more to be concerned about in the broader news milieu than the knowing dissemination of false information with a deceptive purpose. Indeed, the successful propagation and extensive influence of fake news hint at a deeper concern, one demonstrating a woeful lack of media literacy among news consumers and, perhaps even more broadly, insufficient information literacy skills in society.

It is no surprise, then, that librarians have taken up the cause of how to teach readers to identify fake news and prevent it from spreading. A number of articles have covered the role of librarians in dealing with this issue (e.g., Banks 2016; Higgins DeSmet 2017). One example of an action that librarians can take is the creation of a news research guide. Many such guides have been created on the LibGuides platform. LibGuides is a content management system created by Springshare. It allows for the easy compilation of library resources, simplifying the process of creating research guides. The guides are hosted on the cloud and available to the broader LibGuides community, but they can also be integrated into a library's existing Web site for a seamless user experience. A simple search in the LibGuides community yields more than 4,000 individual pages that mention the phrase "fake news." These come from a variety of libraries, but the overwhelming majority are in academic libraries.

Fake news and its root causes might connect easily with academic librarians because of the centralization of information literacy by their primary professional organization, the Association of College and Research Libraries (ACRL). Through the *Framework for Information Literacy in Higher Education*, ACRL emphasizes issues of information literacy as a core concern of the profession (ACRL Board 2017). This chapter focuses on the potential benefits for academic librarians of using the topical issue of fake news to address the central concern for improving literacy across all types of information. It also provides ideas for using existing LibGuides to teach students about information literacy and evaluates a number of existing LibGuides related to the topic of fake news.

FAKE NEWS AS GATEWAY TO INFORMATION LITERACY

This term "fake news" has frequently been overused and misapplied. Many have used it as a catchall for any questionable or biased reporting, and there has been some conflation with satirical news (Tandoc, Lim, and Ling 2017). In this chapter, "fake news" refers to stories that are based on false information and written with deceptive intentions, generally with the goal of getting clicks to generate ad revenue or to create partisan influence (Sydell 2016). Issues of bias or authority are important to pay attention to as well.

Of course, evaluating news sources is far from the only situation that necessitates the use of information literacy skills. As ACRL defines the concept, "Information literacy is the set of integrated abilities encompassing the reflective discovery of information, the understanding of how information is produced and valued, and the use of information in creating new knowledge and participating ethically in communities of learning" (ACRL 2017). Information literacy skills can be used in understanding and evaluating a variety of sources in different contexts.

Why focus on fake news to promote better information literacy? The topical nature of fake news and its enduring relevance facilitates student understanding of the importance of information literacy skills in everyday situations and in academic contexts. Jillian Powers, Ann Musgrove, and Lauri Rebar noted that using the topic of fake news to teach information literacy can be especially effective with Millennial undergraduate students, who often lack the ability to successfully navigate the digital information landscape and make critical judgments of their findings (Powers, Musgrove, and Rebar 2017). These authors see this approach as best used in conjunction with LibGuides, a Web-based platform that allows for easier access to e-resources.

One recent example that follows this model is the popular "Beyoncé's Lemonade and Information Resources" guide by Jenny Ferretti at the Maryland Institute College of Art (http://libguides.mica.edu/lemonade). Ferretti focuses on Beyoncé's *Lemonade* visual album as a way to "engage students through a popular point of reference" (2016 n.p.). She shares articles and books that relate to different aspects of the album, including literature, art, women's studies, critical race theory, and history. Even without explicitly referring to information literacy, Ferretti still manages to get at many of its core aspects by sharing the scholarly conversation surrounding the album and encouraging further research into various related subjects. The popularity of this particular guide, which was viewed 14,000 times in the first 24 hours alone, speaks to the potential success of conveying the importance of information literacy through topical issues such as popular art and music and, perhaps most effectively, fake news.

Still, the connection between fake news and teaching nuanced, thoughtful information literacy is not necessarily a given. Early reactions to the spread of fake news after the 2016 U.S. presidential election focused on providing checklists and other simple tools that were useful in addressing general concerns about news authenticity. These tools included lists of Web sites known to disseminate fake news, browser plug-ins that alerted users to questionable news stories, and fact-checking Web sites that researched stories floating around the Internet. These tools can be useful resources and are certainly worth sharing. As shortcuts for identifying fake news, they can appeal to students who may be looking for simple solutions. However, they do not help students develop their source evaluation skills, and they can obscure other issues students should be aware of when evaluating information, such as bias. By focusing on educating students to be able to identify fake news on their own, librarians can teach them improved critical thinking and information literacy skills.

TAKING ACTION WITH RESEARCH GUIDES

As previously noted, many academic librarians have already taken up the cause of fake news and are working toward helping students understand how to identify it. One method of doing so has been to create research guides through LibGuides. These guides take many forms and go into varying degrees of detail. Some are simple, one-page guides that list other resources and tools available across the Web for identifying fake news. Others offer checklists to follow in evaluating news sources but offer limited information literacy instruction. Few guides present ways of improving broader source evaluation skills and drawing connections to information literacy.

Other guides take slightly different approaches to focusing on news and information literacy, thus hinting at the many possible permutations of focusing on this topic and its adaptability to different styles of research guides. For example, the Temple University Libraries offer a guide titled "Information Literacy in an Era of Alternative Facts and Fake News" (De Voe n.d.). It largely retains a focus on fake news, but introduces students to other important concerns in evaluating sources, such as confirmation bias and filter bubbles, and offers its own set of questions to ask when evaluating sources.

Another useful guide is the Libraries at Florida International University's "Fake News: Read All about It!" (Castillo n.d.). It discusses other types of information sources and provides ways to evaluate all types of online sources. Also useful is the Limestone College's A. J. Eastwood Library's guide (Ward n.d.). It was adapted from the University of Oregon Libraries'

A FAKE NEWS LIBGUIDE FOR UNIVERSITY OF OREGON (UO) LIBRARIES

At the beginning of 2017, at perhaps the height of interest in the fake news problem, there was discussion within UO Libraries about creating a resource for students to help them navigate the ever evolving online news landscape. As the liaison for UO's School of Journalism and Communication (SOJC), I felt I was in the right role to spearhead the creation of this guide. It would be aimed at a broader audience than just SOJC students, as the issue clearly stems from a widespread lack of media literacy and is not specific to any one student group.

Before building the guide, I looked into what other academic libraries had already put together. Some had already created very useful resources that provided tools specifically intended to help identify fake news, as well as checklists that offered easy steps to follow in evaluating news sources. However, I knew I wanted to go beyond this type of guide and draw connections to general source evaluation skills.

The resulting guide was simply titled "Fake News and Information Literacy" (Hernandez n.d.). I consciously structured it so that the focus would move from fake news to general evaluation skills over four individual sections. Readers are welcomed with an introduction to information literacy and an explanation of the connection to fake news. From there, they can find links to practical tools and guides specifically useful for identifying fake news, followed by resources that go beyond the issue of false information to related information evaluation concerns, such as bias. The final section features a set of questions to ask when evaluating any kind of information source, considering the important aspects of authority, objectivity, quality, currency, and relevancy in determining information credibility. This brings things full circle and back to information literacy, reminding students that following these steps is important when consuming any information, whether they are reading the news or researching for a class paper.

guide (https://researchguides.uoregon.edu/fakenews) to fit resources available at their own institution, while also adding another section that guides students on becoming critical readers of online information.

FAKE NEWS WORKSHOPS AND INSTRUCTION SESSIONS

Beyond research guides, instruction sessions and workshops are another useful method for educating undergraduate students about these issues. Whether designed for students enrolled in specific courses or open to broader audiences, these sessions use fake news as a focal point to teach source evaluation skills. While research guides can help students find useful resources to help them in avoiding fake news and other questionable sources, active instructional approaches typically involve hands-on activities that allow the students to work through the process of analyzing the credibility of sources. Having students work through the process while in the same room with a librarian provides them an easier way to ask questions in the moment. The instruction session format can also encourage better understanding of the material, particularly benefitting women and disadvantaged students, thereby helping narrow the achievement gap in the classroom (Haak, HilleRisLambers, Pitre, and Freeman 2011).

For some students, hands-on learning might be more effective than the independent use of guides for making the connection between identifying fake news and the broader skills necessary in evaluating all types of sources. Instruction sessions activities can allow for a more natural side-by-side comparison of how this process could work for different types of sources.

A FAKE NEWS WORKSHOP AT THE UNIVERSITY OF OREGON LIBRARIES

Not long after having created the "Fake News and Information Literacy" research guide, I began planning a workshop that would address the same topic. The idea initially sprang from discussions with faculty members at SOJC, who expressed interest in such a workshop as the issue of fake news became a dominant topic of conversation in the school. Faculty understood that it is just as important for students to learn how to be smart consumers of news as it is for them to learn how to create online content.

In planning the core instructional exercise for this session, I wanted it to be adaptable. As instructors, academic librarians are often working in different teaching environments, sometimes in rooms with computers, sometimes without, and sometimes in online classes. With that in mind, I designed an activity based around the guide I had already created (https://researchguides.uoregon.edu/fakenews). After introducing students to the guide, I could divide them into groups or pairs, depending on the number of students. Each group would receive a few different news articles of varying levels of credibility, as well as discussion questions to work through as they evaluated the articles. Using the evaluation questions from the guide, they would evaluate the articles and decide whether they believed them to be credible. After all groups had a chance to complete the evaluation task, the class would come back together and work through follow-up discussion questions.

Another example of a fake news library class guide comes from Western State Colorado University. "Manipulation and Misdirection in the Media" (Leslie J. Savage Library, n.d.) also centers on a research guide but integrates the evaluation activity directly into it. After introducing the guide to the students, they are split into four groups and directed to follow the tasks for their respective group. Each group has a different scenario leading them through the process of evaluating different information types or finding more information on a particular source. Upon completion of the tasks, each group then presents their scenario and the process they followed in working on it.

CONCLUSION

Concern about fake news does not seem likely to die down any time soon. Many students may not realize it, but they need to be able to effectively evaluate all types of information resources. However, it is not always easy to lead undergraduate students to understand the importance of such skills. By using the topic of fake news to show students the immediate relevance of information literacy, academic librarians are finding an effective way to introduce students to these concepts. Through research guides and instruction sessions, they are encouraging students not just to improve their skills in identifying fake news but also to draw connections to evaluating all types of information in their research. Not only does this approach enables students to develop their skills in topical concerns but also, more broadly, it will benefit them in the long run.

REFERENCES

ACRL Board. "Framework for Information Literacy for Higher Education." Association of College and Research Libraries (ACRL), 11 January 2016. http://www.ala.org/acrl/standards/ilframework.

Ansari, Talal, and Jane Lytvynenko. "Here Is the Misinformation Going around about the Texas Church Shooting." BuzzFeed, 6 November 2017. https://www.buzzfeed.com/talalansari/fake-news -about-the-texas-church-shooting?utm_term=.ve44OZjmw#.gcG MyePwD.

Banks, Marcus. "Fighting Fake News: How Libraries Can Lead the Way on Media Literacy." American Libraries, 27 December 2016.

https://americanlibrariesmagazine.org/2016/12/27/fighting-fake
-news/.

Castillo, Melissa Del. "Fake News: Read All about It! Fake News," n.d.
http://libguides.fiu.edu/fakenews.

De Voe, Kristina. "Information Literacy in an Era of Alternative Facts
and Fake News." Temple University, n.d. http://guides.temple
.edu/fakenews.

Ferretti, Jenny. "Beyoncé's Lemonade—The LibGuide Heard Round the
(twitter)World" Springshare, 18 May 2016. https://blog.springshare
.com/2016/05/18/beyonces-lemonade-the-libguide-heard-round
-the-twitterworld/.

Google Trends. "Fake News—Explore," n.d. https://trends.google.com
/trends/explore?q=fake news#TIMESERIES.

Haak, David C., Janneke HilleRisLambers, Emile Pitre, and Scott Freeman.
"Increased Structure and Active Learning Reduce the Achievement
Gap in Introductory Biology." *Science* 332, no. 6034 (3 June 2011):
1213–1216. http://science.sciencemag.org/content/332/6034/1213
.abstract.

Hernandez, Carolina. "Fake News and Information Literacy: Introduction,"
n.d. https://researchguides.uoregon.edu/fakenews.

Higgins DeSmet, Nicole. "School Librarians Teach CRAAP to Fight Fake
News." *Burlington Free Press*, 24 July 2017. https://www.usatoday
.com/story/news/nation-now/2017/07/25/school-librarians-teach
-craap-fight-fake-news/507105001/.

Leslie J. Savage Library. "Manipulation and Misdirection in the Media."
Western State Colorado University, n.d. http://library.western.edu
/friendly.php?s=fakenews.

Powers, Jillian, Ann Musgrove, and Lauri Rebar. "Creative Applications
of LibGuides to Teach Undergraduate Students Information Literacy Skills." In *Society for Information Technology & Teacher Education International Conference*, 1407–1413. Waynesville, NC:
Association for the Advancement of Computing in Education
(AACE), 2017. https://www.learntechlib.org/noaccess/177424/.

Sydell, Laura. "We Tracked Down a Fake-News Creator in the Suburbs.
Here's What We Learned." *All Tech Considered*, 23 November 2016.
https://www.npr.org/sections/alltechconsidered/2016/11/23
/503146770/npr-finds-the-head-of-a-covert-fake-news-operation-in
-the-suburbs.

Tandoc Jr., Edson C., Zheng Wei Lim, and Richard Ling. "Defining 'Fake News': A Typology of Scholarly Definitions." *Digital Journalism*, 6, no. 2 (2017): 137–153. https://doi.org/10.1080/21670811.2017.1360143.

Ward, Janet. "Fake News and Information Literacy." Limestone College, n.d. http://libguides.limestone.edu/fakenews.

About the Editor and Contributors

Denise E. Agosto, PhD, is professor in the College of Computing & Informatics at Drexel University and director of Drexel's Master of Library and Information Science program. An active library educator and promoter for over 20 years, she researches young people's use of social technologies and how public library services can support users' information needs.

In addition to her current position as professor and librarian for the University of Rhode Island Libraries, **Joanna M. Burkhardt** has taught information literacy to students and teachers for nearly 20 years. She holds an MA in anthropology from the University of Wisconsin–Madison and an MLS from the University of Rhode Island.

Associate professor **Nicole A. Cooke**, PhD, serves as program director for the Master of Library and Information Science program at the School of Information Sciences, University of Illinois, Urbana–Champaign. A frequent speaker at state and national conferences, Dr. Cooke's research and teaching explore online information behaviors, critical cultural information studies, and diversity and social justice in librarianship.

A tireless champion for media literacy education in schools, **Belinha De Abreu**, PhD, is an international expert to the Forum on Partnerships on Media & Information Literacy for UNESCO's Communication & Information Section, vice president for the National Telemedia Council, and a member of the Leadership Council for the National Association for Media

Literacy Education. Dr. De Abreu has written/edited five books on the topic of media literacy, with work on a sixth book underway.

Shevon Desai is the communication studies and information science librarian at the University of Michigan (U-M) Library, where she works with faculty and students to provide research and instructional support for the Communication Studies Department and the School of Information. A member of the U-M Library staff since 2004, Shevon also selects materials related to news and general periodicals.

Kristina M. De Voe is English and communication librarian at Temple University. She holds an MLIS from Kent State University, and her research interests revolve around the intersections of information/media literacy and scholarly communication, plus digital rhetoric and the canon of memory.

Carolina Hernandez is the journalism and communication librarian at the University of Oregon Libraries in Eugene, Oregon. She received an MLIS from the University of Wisconsin–Madison and an MA in Media Studies from the University of Texas at Austin.

As a librarian at White Plains Public Library, in White Plains, New York, **Ben Himmelfarb** specializes in local history and community programming. He holds master's degrees in history and information science from the State University of New York at Albany.

Kay Mathiesen, PhD, is associate professor in the School of Information at the University of Arizona in Tucson. Her research combines a background in philosophy with epistemic examinations of information ethics and justice.

School library media director **Kristen Mattson**, EdD, oversees the library at Waubonsie Valley High School in Aurora, Illinois. Dr. Mattson is also a frequent writer on the topics of digital citizenship, educational innovation, instructional technology, and Future Ready Libraries.

Sharon McQueen, PhD, is an award-winning historian, biographer, and educator. Her research examines sociocultural aspects of children's literature, and her forthcoming book explores the creation and phenomenal reception of the 1936 U.S. picture book *The Story of Ferdinand*.

Hailey Mooney works at the University of Michigan as the psychology and sociology librarian. She holds a BA in sociology from the University of Michigan and an MLS from Wayne State University.

Jo Angela Oehrli serves as learning librarian/children's literature librarian at the University of Michigan Library in Ann Arbor. As a former high school and middle school teacher, Angie uses her teaching background and master of science in information from the University of Michigan to help students locate, evaluate, and apply information of all types.

Shannon M. Oltmann, PhD, is an associate professor in the College of Communication and Information, School of Information Science, at the University of Kentucky at Lexington. Her research focuses on access to information, intellectual freedom and censorship, information policy, privacy, and public libraries.

Caitlin Shanley is the instruction team leader and liaison librarian for American Studies, Asian Studies, and Gender, Sexuality, and Women's Studies at Temple University and an adjunct faculty librarian at the Community College of Philadelphia. She holds an MSLS from University of North Carolina–Chapel Hill, and her research interests revolve around gender, sexuality, and creative approaches to teaching and learning in libraries.

Well-known around the world as a champion of libraries and literacy, **Julie B. Todaro**, DLS, is the dean of Library Services at Austin Community College in Austin, Texas. In addition to having worked as a library manager and educator for more than 40 years, Dr. Todaro served as the 2016–2017 president of the American Library Association.

Mark Winston, PhD, is the executive director of the J. Lewis Crozer Library in Chester, Pennsylvania, and he has also served as a management consultant and trainer, academic library director, and teaching faculty member. His research and publications focus on various aspects of leadership, diversity, ethics, access to information, and economic inequality.

Index